EQUIPPED FOR
PEACE
Tools For Your Calling

LEAH BOATRIGHT

Editor: Jerilyn Schrock

LCCN: 2025906162
ISBN: 979-8-9916836-0-9

Contents

Forward

This book was born from a desire to see the Bride of Christ equipped to walk in His peace. As I began writing, Hebrews 13:20-21 (NIV) became my guiding light: *"Now may the God of peace... equip you with everything good for doing His will, and may He work in us what is pleasing to Him, through Jesus Christ."* Through these pages, I pray you'll find the strength and courage to walk in His peace and fulfill His calling.

This verse reflects my prayer for you to be equipped to walk in God's peace and live His will. As you journey through these pages, may you experience His peace in a way that strengthens and empowers you for the calling He has placed on your life.

Acknowledgements

First and foremost, I thank my Lord and Savior, Jesus Christ, the Prince of Peace, whose peace surpasses all understanding and whose love continually guides, equips, and sustains me. Without His grace, this book would not have come to life. It is only through Him that these words have been written.

To my dear friend and editor, Jerilyn Schrock, thank you for your incredible help in making this book a reality. Your guidance and expertise have been invaluable in shaping this work.

Thank you to all those who have supported me and whose unwavering belief in me has been a constant source of strength.

To Thierry Nakoa, thank you for the wisdom and insights you shared through your teachings.

Finally, to the Bride of Christ—may these words help you find strength in His peace and the courage to live out His calling

Introduction

Peace in My Storm

It all began with a painful realization: My joy was gone. Over time, hurt, anger, and exhaustion had gradually smothered it, trapping me in a cycle of constant striving. The joy of the Lord, which was meant to be my strength, felt distant and unreachable. Negative people and difficult circumstances seemed to have taken control of my heart. But as I reflected, I realized I had unknowingly agreed with lies rooted in old wounds, allowing them to influence my actions. Yet, deep within, I knew God's peace and joy were meant to be my true source of strength.

In a world filled with chaos and burdens, I reached a breaking point where reading the Word wasn't enough—I needed to live it. Ephesians 3:19 became my desperate prayer:

to know the love of Christ not only in my mind but in a life-transforming, personal way. He promises His love surpasses knowledge and will fill every part of our being. He doesn't just offer understanding; He invites us into the fullness of His presence.

I cried, "Lord, help me live Your Word, not just read it!" I longed for an authentic and fruitful relationship with Him. This book is the story of that journey and what I discovered along the way.

Finding peace and joy in today's world can feel impossible. Life's storms seem relentless, and the weight of daily burdens and crises can be overwhelming. But deep down, I knew—even though I wasn't yet living it—that we weren't meant to carry these burdens alone. This disconnect led me to wrestle with some hard questions:

- How do we remain unshaken in the midst of chaos?

- How can we stay grounded in the fruit of the Spirit when everything seems to be falling apart?

- How do we walk in the peace Jesus promised?

These questions sparked a journey that transformed me. As I sought God, He revealed profound truths about Himself and the condition of my heart. I learned that peace and joy are not things we strive for or earn; they are gifts woven into our covenant with Jesus. They flow naturally out of our relationship with Him.

God also revealed the roots of my struggles—people-pleasing and the fear of man. I realized I had spent much of my life seeking validation from others, trying to meet expectations, and fearing rejection. These patterns had kept me trapped for years. But as I invited God into the healing process, He began to mend my wounds. Through inner healing, His grace brought true renewal—restoring my heart, reviving my overall well-being, and deepening my connection with Him. As a result, I began to live with greater peace and joy.

I learned that living peaceably with everyone, as described in Romans 12:18, doesn't mean avoiding conflict or losing yourself to please others. It's about living from a whole heart and seeking unity, no matter the circumstances. This journey required overcoming limiting beliefs, healing from trauma, and addressing the weight of unforgiveness.

I have always been a peacemaker, but only recently did I fully understand the significance of this calling. The insights I've gained are woven throughout these pages. Being a peacemaker is a profound blessing. As Matthew 5:9 states: *"Blessed are the peacemakers, for they shall be called sons of God."*

My heart has always been to help others reconcile with God and one another, cultivating peace through the Holy Spirit's guidance. This desire to bring unity led me to counseling and life coaching, where I've witnessed the power of God's peace at work. I long for a world where His peace touches every life.

This book is also rooted in Hebrews 13:20-21: *"Now the God of peace... make you perfect in every good work to do His will, working in you that which is well-pleasing in His sight, through Jesus Christ."* I pray that these lessons will strengthen and equip you for His calling.

I found that navigating life alone left me feeling lost in my journey. In the chaos of my struggles, I realized my deep need to rely entirely on God. By leaning into His strength and wisdom, I discovered the path He had laid before me—one I could never have seen on my own. God's glory is always accessible to us, but we must draw from it, just as branches draw life from the vine. As we remain steadfast in our commitment to Him, His life flows through us, transforming us into reflections of His love and power.

On my path to healing, I have understood that being a peacemaker isn't just about helping others—it begins within. I have realized that true peace comes from a deep relationship with God, just as a bride's voice reflects the intimacy of her connection with the King. It is in this closeness with God that true peace and transformation happen.

God calls us to be overcomers and to remain rooted in Him. He has provided us with everything we need, but we must depend on Him entirely. We can be purified, healed, and strengthened in our relationship with Him. Those who are willing to surrender will be rewarded. He is waiting for our "YES."

Yes, you will face tests and trials, but through them, you will know that you are indeed His and begin to experience the depths of His power. Whether you have already faced testing, are in the midst of it, or will also face it in the future, a time will come when you will be ready to rise to your calling—walking as Jesus walked and embracing His assignment for you.

I want to guide you in discovering peace for yourself, understanding its depth, and equipping you to walk in peace daily, no matter what life brings. I share these lessons not because I have it all together but because I deeply desire to help the Bride of Christ be ready—to live in His peace, stand firm, and walk as Jesus did. As we move through the lessons God has taught me, I hope you'll gain fresh understanding, knowing there's always more to learn and opportunities for growth.

As you progress through these pages, bring everything before the Lord with an open heart. Healing takes time and intentionality, so be patient with yourself. If something stirs a negative emotional reaction—a trigger—bring it to Jesus and trust in His grace to heal what needs restoration.

By triggers, I mean emotional or psychological reactions sparked by certain words, situations, or memories. These reactions can resurface past pain or distress, often making emotions feel more significant than the present moment. If

LEAH BOATRIGHT

you experience a trigger, it may be a sign that God is inviting you into deeper healing.

I pray that the words in this book and my experiences allow the Lord to heal your heart. There is no shame in the process—only growth, peace, and a deeper intimacy with Him. See appendix A

This book has the potential to help guide you into a life far more fulfilling than you ever imagined. Being equipped for peace means you already have what you need to walk confidently in God's plan. It's about standing firm in His peace, no matter the circumstances.

Let's walk through this together and discover the incredible life God has in store for you!

Cover:

We featured a barefoot person on the cover because it is a powerful symbol. Walking barefoot signifies humility, surrender, and deep connection, reflecting a heart fully yielded to God. It reminds us that peace comes when we step out of our strength and walk in His. Barefoot, we tread lightly, mindful of each step, just as we are called to walk intentionally and in harmony with the Spirit. This image invites us to embrace authenticity and vulnerability and learn to walk in God's peace.

6

One

The Journey to Peace

Life can feel like a whirlwind, relentlessly toss-
ing us from one challenge to the next. That
was my reality—everything unraveled at once,
leaving me feeling hopeless and overwhelmed.

The job I had poured my heart into was gone, leaving me
questioning my purpose and identity. At home, the laughter
and connection that once filled our family were replaced by
silence and tension. My marriage felt distant—two people
living separate lives under the same roof- and my adult

children were making heartbreaking choices that I couldn't control.

Each day felt heavier than the last, and I wondered how much longer I could hold it all together. In that season of brokenness, I cried out to God with a raw and desperate plea: "God, I can't do this anymore. I need You!" Though I didn't have the answers, I sensed His presence in the silence. Slowly, as I surrendered my pain and confusion to Him, He began to heal my heart.

Amid life's storms, the presence of Jesus becomes more than just a place of refuge; it becomes the foundation upon which we stand. When we allow ourselves to be secure in Him, we discover a peace that isn't dependent on the shifting tides of our circumstances. He gave me more than just comfort; He gave me something deeper—His peace. And this peace didn't come because the storms of my life ceased; they raged on. It came because I encountered the Prince of Peace Himself. I found an anchor in His presence that held me steady in the chaos.

As we walk through life's challenges, the promise of peace in Philippians 4:7 shines brightly: *"And the peace of God, which surpasses all understanding, will guard your hearts and minds through Christ Jesus."* This is not a superficial calm or a temporary relief. It is a peace transcending human logic, guarding our hearts and minds through Christ's presence and power. He does not just give us peace; He is our peace, walking us through fractured relationships, overwhelming circumstances, and the deepest valleys of life.

But what happens when we feel distant from this peace? Often, it reveals areas of our hearts where we have yet to experience its truth and fully believe in its transformative power. These moments highlight where the Holy Spirit desires to work within us, restoring and reconciling what is broken. Peace begins as a deeply personal journey—an invitation to allow God to fill the voids, heal the wounds, and help us experience His love and truth in a way that surpasses mere knowledge. This transformative power of peace gives us hope and inspires us to grow spiritually.

The Hard and Holy Work of Peacemaking

While peace is a gift, living in it requires intentionality. True peace—Shalom—isn't passive. It requires courage, surrender, and a willingness to reflect God's heart in our relationships and circumstances. Peacemaking is not simply the absence of conflict but the active presence of God's love, wisdom, and restoration at work in us.

This active role in peacemaking empowers us and reminds us of our daily responsibility to reflect God's love and peace. As Jesus declared: *"Blessed are the peacemakers, for they shall be called sons of God"* (Matthew 5:9).

Peacemaking is not just about de-escalating conflict. It's about actively pursuing reconciliation, even when it's difficult. At times, it involves purposefully and prayerfully stepping into conflict resolution. Ephesians 2:14 reminds us that Christ Himself is our peace—breaking down the walls that divide us.

If He has reconciled us to God, we are called to reflect that same reconciliation in our relationships: *"For He Himself is our peace, who has made both one and has broken down the middle wall of separation"* (Ephesians 2:14).

Christ is the ultimate bridge to wholeness, and we are called to be conduits of His peace. James 3:18 affirms that true righteousness flourishes in peace and is cultivated by those who intentionally pursue it. Peacemaking is a spiritual discipline that bears fruit in our lives and the lives of others: *"Now the fruit of righteousness is sown in peace by those who make peace"* (James 3:18).

This active role in peacemaking empowers us and reminds us of our daily responsibility to reflect God's love and peace. As Jesus declared: *"Blessed are the peacemakers, for they shall be called sons of God"* (Matthew 5:9).

Peacemaking doesn't mean we must agree with everyone; it means actively choosing peace, even when it's difficult to agree. It requires surrender and letting go of our ego to preserve a connection. In those moments, we must ask ourselves: How can we reflect Christ in this situation? What do I need to give up or sacrifice to maintain a connection here? We mirror Christ's sacrificial love as we engage in this holy work. Colossians 3:13 calls us to a deeper level of peacemaking—one rooted in forgiveness. Just as Christ forgave us, we are called to extend that same grace to others, even when it's difficult: *"Bearing with one another, and forgiving one another, if anyone has a complaint against another; even as Christ forgave you, so you also must do"* (Colossians 3:13).

This work of peacemaking isn't always easy, but it is holy. When we forgive, pursue reconciliation, and choose love over bitterness, we create space for God's Shalom to thrive. There are moments when His yoke truly feels effortless, and grace fills the gap in those moments, making the heavy burdens light.

Yet, as followers of Christ, we are called to die to our flesh and surrender completely to Him. Are there areas of your life that have not fully yielded to Him? Where do you need to let go and submit to His will? If we're not living from a place of peace, we get to dig in and discover what part of our flesh refuses to let go.

If we claim to belong to Christ, we must walk as those who have crucified the flesh. True transformation comes when we lay it all at His feet, allowing Him to shape us into His likeness. Only then can we truly live as peacemakers, reflecting His glory in a broken world.

Living as Ambassadors of Peace

We are called to be messengers of peace in a world filled with conflict. As those who have committed to Christ—believing in Him and actively participating in His mission—we must align ourselves with His teachings, follow His example, and reflect His love and peace.

2 Corinthians 5:18-19 reminds us that God has entrusted us with the ministry of reconciliation. We are not just recipients of His peace; we are His ambassadors, chosen to bring His kingdom of peace into a broken world.

"Now all things are of God, who has reconciled us to Himself through Jesus Christ and has given us the ministry of reconciliation, that is, that God was in Christ reconciling the world to Himself, not imputing their trespasses to them, and has committed to us the word of reconciliation" (2 Corinthians 5:18-19).

Being an ambassador of peace doesn't mean we won't face challenges. It means we decide to respond differently by embracing Christ's love rather than reacting based on our emotions, past wounds, or flawed examples of the world. We choose:

- Forgiveness over bitterness

- Compassion over judgment

- Humility over pride

Living as a peacemaker is about more than avoiding conflict—it's about allowing God's peace to flow through us and transform the atmosphere around us. It requires daily surrender to Him, seeking His will over our desires, and asking, "Lord, how do You want me to respond in this moment?"

When we embrace this calling, we don't just receive peace—we release it. We become carriers of God's peace through our words, actions, and how we love. We are His hands and feet, bringing hope and healing wherever we go.

This is not just a personal blessing but a holy and weighty calling. This world is desperate for peace, and as ambassadors of Christ, we are uniquely positioned to reflect His glory and commissioned to bring heaven's restoration to earth.

The Source of Our Peace

God is the ultimate *"God of Peace,"* a title Paul frequently uses in his letters. Romans 15:33 declares, *"Now the God of peace be with you all."* This verse reassures us that peace is not something we can manufacture ourselves—it flows directly from God Himself.

The writer of Hebrews further emphasizes this truth, drawing from the Greek word for peace, which finds its root in the Hebrew word shalom. Unlike the world's superficial definition of peace as merely the absence of conflict, shalom encompasses wholeness, completeness, and the fullness of God's blessings. It signifies every good thing God provides—physically, spiritually, mentally, and emotionally.

God is the source and sustainer of this supernatural peace, embodying its essence throughout eternity—past, present, and future. He fulfilled its promise through Jesus Christ: "For He Himself is our peace" (Ephesians 2:14). Not only did Jesus embody peace, but He also freely gave it to us as a precious gift: *"Peace I leave with you: My peace I give to you"* (John 14:27).

For generations, humanity has searched for peace apart from God. However, worldly peace is temporary, just fleeting moments of relief. True peace can only be found in God, for He alone is its Creator and Source.

Romans 16:20 reveals that the God of Peace is not passive but mighty and victorious: *"The God of peace will crush Satan under your feet shortly."* This truth assures us that God's peace is not weak but a conquering peace. It defeats evil, silences opposition, and establishes God's reign. Through Christ, this peace triumphs over Satan and all forces of darkness, bringing lasting victory and divine resolution. His peace empowers believers to walk in authority, share in His triumph, and vanquish even the greatest forces of evil.

Paul reinforces this in Philippians 4:9: *"The things which you learned and received and heard and saw in me, these do, and the God of peace will be with you."* When we embrace God's peace, it does more than calm our hearts; it restores us from within, aligning us with His will and empowering us to walk in His ways. 1 Thessalonians 5:23 affirms this transforming work: *"Now may the God of peace Himself sanctify you completely; and may your whole spirit, soul, and body be preserved blameless at the coming of our Lord Jesus Christ."*

When we center our lives on Him, our entire being—body, soul, and spirit—finds the wholeness we seek. As Psalm 119:165 declares: *"Great peace have those who love Your law, and nothing causes them to stumble."*

By agreeing with God's ways, we experience His profound peace, which holds us steady through every season.

As we step into each day, may our lives reflect God's peace so clearly that others are drawn to Him and say about us, "You are just like your Heavenly Father."

Peace is not just a gift we receive—it is an inheritance we claim and a calling we embrace as His ambassadors.

May the God of Peace empower you to accomplish what feels impossible. May He fill you with His Spirit of Peace, enabling you to glorify Him in all you do. And as you rely on the One who authors peace, may He equip you to carry it, live it, and become a testimony of His unshakable peace.

Conclusion

As we have seen, peace is more than the absence of conflict; Shalom is the fullness of God's presence in every part of our lives. It's not a passive state but an active pursuit, requiring us to align our hearts, minds, and actions with God's Word and His Spirit.

Peace is a daily choice, a continual surrender to the Lord as our Source, allowing Him to fill us with His presence. God's peace is complete well-being, wholeness, and harmony encompassing every aspect of our lives. When we surrender to Him and walk in alignment with His will, we don't just receive peace; we become carriers of it,

Shalom doesn't stop at personal peace. The peace of God working in and through us creates a ripple effect that extends to our relationships, communities, and, ultimately, the world.

In the next chapter, we will continue exploring the depth of Shalom and examine the unshakable covenant that anchors it.

Two

The Covenant that Changes Everything

Peace is found in Jesus Christ, who invites us
into a New Covenant that transforms our hearts,
reshapes our identity, and empowers us to live
in victorious freedom through His unwavering
grace.

What is a covenant?

In Scripture, a covenant is far more than a contract or
agreement; it is a sacred and binding relationship initiated

and upheld by God. Unlike human agreements, which are often conditional and subject to failure, a covenant reflects God's eternal and unshakable commitment to His people.

The word covenant carries the weight of divine intention. It represents a solemn, eternal pledge grounded not in human effort but in God's unwavering faithfulness. Hebrews 6:17-18 highlights the unchanging nature of God's promise:

"God also bound Himself with an oath so that those who received the promise could be perfectly sure that He would never change His mind. So, God has given both His promise and His oath. These two things are unchangeable because it is impossible for God to lie. Therefore, we who have fled to Him for refuge can have great confidence as we hold to the hope that lies before us."

This assurance underscores the beauty of God's covenants: they are not dependent on our strength or ability but are rooted in His character and love.

The Promise Fulfilled in Christ

The New Covenant, prophesied in Jeremiah 31:31-34, was God's promise to establish a deeply personal and transformative relationship with His people: *"I will put my law in their inward parts, and write it in their hearts, and will be their God, and they shall be my people."*

Jesus Christ fulfilled this profound covenant promise. As the mediator of the New Covenant, His death and resurrection bridged the gap between God and humanity. Through His sacrifice, He ushers in a peace that surpasses circumstances, bringing reconciliation, restoration, and an abiding relationship with the Father. Isaiah 9:6 calls Jesus the *"Prince of Peace,"* signifying His mission to restore what was broken.

This truth is powerfully echoed in Ephesians 2:14–16, (NLT): *"For Christ Himself has brought peace to us. He united Jews and Gentiles into one people when, in His own body on the cross, He broke down the wall of hostility that separated us. He did this by ending the system of law with its commandments and regulations. He made peace between Jews and Gentiles by creating in Himself one new people from the two groups. Together as one body, Christ reconciled both groups to God by means of His death on the cross, and our hostility toward each other was put to death."*

In the New Covenant, Jesus dismantles division and hostility, offering unity through His Spirit. The essence of this Covenant of Peace is reconciliation—with God and with others—through Christ.

Living in the Reality of the Covenant

The New Covenant is not about human striving but divine thriving. In Christ, we are made entirely new, empowered by the indwelling Holy Spirit to live lives of fulfillment and peace. As 2 Corinthians 5:17 declares: *"Therefore, if anyone is in Christ, he is a new creation; old things have passed away; behold, all things have become new."*

This covenant in Christ goes beyond external rituals and commands; it focuses on renewing the heart and mind. As God declares in Ezekiel 36:26: *"I will give you a new heart and put a new spirit within you; I will take the heart of stone out of your flesh and give you a heart of flesh."*

This divine exchange equips us to walk in holiness, faith, and peace. Romans 8:11 affirms the Spirit's power within us: *"But if the Spirit of Him who raised Jesus from the dead dwells in you, He who raised Christ from the dead will also give life to your mortal bodies through His Spirit who dwells in you."*

Through the Holy Spirit, we are assured of God's promises and empowered to live in their reality, including the peace declared in Isaiah 54:10: *"For the mountains shall depart and the hills be removed, but My kindness shall not depart from you, nor shall My covenant of peace be removed,"* says the Lord, who has mercy on you.

Faith: Our Response to the New Covenant

The New Covenant is God's invitation to live in peace, wholeness, and fulfillment through Christ. However, it requires our active response: faith. Faith is not merely intellectual agreement; it is trust in action, rooted in God's character and the truth of His Word. Although God initiated and upholds the covenant, we are called to respond in faith, aligning our hearts and lives with His promises.

Faith Grows Through the Word

Faith is not something we muster on our own; it comes from hearing and believing God's Word. Romans 10:17 says: *"So then faith comes by hearing, and hearing by the word of God."*

God's Word reveals His nature, promises, covenant, and faithfulness. As we immerse ourselves in Scripture, our understanding deepens, and our trust in Him strengthens.

Faith is Refined Through Trials

Faith is not built in times of ease but is refined and strengthened through the challenges and hardships of life, much like metal is purified in the intense heat of a crucible. James 1:3-4 reminds us: *"Knowing that the testing of your faith produces patience. But let patience have its perfect work, that you may be perfect and complete, lacking nothing."*

During our difficulties, we have the opportunity to trust God more deeply. These moments test and refine our faith, producing endurance and maturity. Even when doubt creeps in, God's grace meets us right where we are. Like the man in Mark 9:24, we can cry out: *"Lord, I believe; help my unbelief!"*

This honest prayer invites God to strengthen our faith and guide us into deeper trust.

Faith is the Gateway to Peace

Faith gives us access to the peace of the New Covenant. Romans 5:1 states: *"Therefore, having been justified by faith, we have peace with God through our Lord Jesus Christ."*

Faith bridges the gap between our human limitations and God's divine provision. It enables us to enter the victory and rest that Jesus has already secured. This peace is not merely a fleeting feeling nor the lack of running away from confrontation; instead, it is found in the person of Jesus Christ. It is the assurance that God is with us, for us, and working all things together for our good (Romans 8:28).

Faith allows us to experience the fullness of God's peace. Through faith, we trust in His promises, stand firm in His truth, and silence the voice of fear. Without faith, peace remains distant—an idea rather than a reality. But when we anchor our faith in Jesus, we are no longer tossed by the waves of circumstance; we stand upon the Rock that cannot be shaken.

I remember a time when I struggled with doubt. I had been praying for many years, yet my prayers seemed to go unanswered. Not only was I not seeing any fruit—not even a bud—but things got worse. I didn't think that was even possible. My family, who had once avoided dealing with things, suddenly began expressing anger and blame. Years of buried unforgiveness surfaced, and even threats were spoken from places of deep hurt.

I was devastated. How could this have happened when I was doing everything I knew to do, I mean, everything! I prayed, fasted, declared Scripture, worshipped, and sought wise counsel. But nothing changed. Then, in exhaustion, I agreed with a lie: Why bother? Nothing was working.

That's when the Lord opened my eyes to Romans 4:5: *"But to him who does not work but believes on Him who justifies the ungodly, his faith is accounted for righteousness."*

I realized I had been trying to make things happen through my own efforts, measuring my peace by my actions instead of trusting in Him. But God wasn't asking me to fix the situation—He was asking me to stand firm and believe. Not through striving or relying on my own understanding, but through obedience, grounded in faith, trusting His promise of new life.

Faith is Trusting the Promises

Faith is more than belief; it is a deep, unwavering trust in God's promises. Hebrews 11 provides countless examples of those who demonstrated faith in action:

- Abraham trusted God's promise and left his home-land, not knowing where he was going.

- Moses, by faith, led the Israelites through the Red

Sea. This was after a night with God's cloud between them and an army trying to kill them, and after Moses stretched out his hand with the rod as God commanded.

- Joshua, by faith, marched around Jericho until the walls fell. The walls didn't fall for six days, but only on the last day after Joshua had obeyed God's command for seven days.

In these and other cases listed in Hebrews 11, faith required a step of obedience, even when the outcome was unseen.

Faith is Anchored in God's Character

The foundation of our faith lies not in what we can do but in God's unchanging nature. Malachi 3:6 reminds us: *"For I am the Lord, I do not change."*

When circumstances shake us, we can rest in the truth that God is faithful, His Word is true, and His promises never fail. Faith is not a solitary endeavor; the Holy Spirit empowers us to trust and obey. Ezekiel 36:27 declares: *"I will put My Spirit within you and cause you to walk in My statutes, and you will keep My judgments and do them."*

With a new heart after Jesus and the same Spirit that raised Him from the dead dwelling in us, the Holy Spirit helps us overcome doubt, guides us into truth, and strengthens our resolve to walk in faith with Him.

Overcoming Lies That Steal Peace:

If faith grants us access to peace, why do so many believers struggle to live in it? Often, it's because we have unknowingly embraced lies that rob us of what is already ours in Christ. The enemy plants seeds of doubt, whispering, "You're not truly at peace. If God were with you, you wouldn't feel this way. True peace means never feeling afraid or uncertain." These lies distort our perspective and keep us bound in fear.

Too many believers struggle to grasp the New Covenant fully because of the lies they've believed—lies regarding their identity, God's faithfulness, and the sufficiency of Christ's sacrifice. These lies create barriers between us and the peace that God promises. But truth has the power to break those barriers down. As John 8:31–32 reminds us, *'If you abide in My word, you are My disciples indeed. And you shall know the truth, and the truth shall make you free.'* To live in the fullness of God's peace, we must expose the lies and replace them with His truth. Ask yourself:

- Do I doubt God's promises in any area of my life?

- Am I striving to earn God's love rather than resting in my identity as His child?

- Is it possible to experience peace, even in my current circumstances?

The thief's mission is clear: to steal, kill, and destroy (John 10:10), but Jesus came to give life and life more abundantly. That includes His peace. In the New Covenant, we are invited to stand firm in God's unshakable peace, even during life's struggles.

The Covenant of Peace is not simply a theological concept but an invitation into a vibrant, ever-deepening relationship with God through Jesus Christ. It offers more than momentary relief—it promises a life anchored in unshakable hope, enduring joy, and supernatural peace. Isaiah 26:3 reminds us: *"You will keep him in perfect peace, whose mind is stayed on You because he trusts in You."*

But peace is not the absence of strife; it is the presence of Christ in the midst of it. Just as Jesus slept through the storm while the disciples panicked, we, too, have a choice—to be shaken by what we see or to rest in Who we know. Peace is not about avoiding life's storms but knowing Who is in the boat with you.

If we aren't experiencing perfect peace, we must examine where our focus lies. Do the worries of this world consume us, or are we rooted in a place of rest, walking with Him and trusting His faithfulness, no matter the circumstances?

How This Became Real to Me

Embracing the New Covenant of Peace requires intentional steps. Before discussing practical ways to align one's life with its promises, I want to share how this truth became real to me.

For me, the covenant truly came alive when I meditated on Jeremiah 33:3: *"Call to Me, and I will answer you and show you great and mighty things which you do not know."*

As I read this verse, it leaped off the page and settled deep in my heart. From that moment on, whenever I cry out to God, I know He hears me and answers. This truth has transformed my relationship with Him, deepened my faith, and empowered me to walk in the promises of the New Covenant every day.

Living in this covenant isn't just about knowing the truth; it's about experiencing it. It's about personally receiving the benefits of this covenant—peace, restoration, and a deeper relationship with God. As I've chosen to apply His Word to my life, I've witnessed His faithfulness unfold in powerful ways. His peace has entered places of turmoil, His restoration has touched the broken areas of my heart, and I've discovered an intimacy with God I never thought possible.

Peace Transforms Every Area of Life

When you embrace the Covenant of Peace, it begins to reshape every aspect of your life:

- In your relationship with God: You are reconciled and made whole, no longer striving but resting in the assurance of His love.

- In your relationship with yourself: You discover your identity as a beloved child of God, free from shame and empowered to walk in victory.

- In your relationships with others: You become a peacemaker, carrying Jesus' heart into your family, community, and beyond.

God's peace equips you to reflect His love in a world desperate for hope. It empowers you to rise above fear, speak truth in love, and extend grace even in conflict. Jesus said in John 14:27: *"Peace I leave with you, My peace I give to you; not as the world gives do I give to you; let not your heart be troubled, neither let it be afraid."*

This is the peace of God—not the kind of peace the world offers, fleeting and fragile, but the unshakable, perfect peace of the Creator of the universe. He's offering it to you. Will you receive it? Will you let His peace guard your heart and mind?

You don't need to fear the responsibility of carrying God's peace. It is not your peace that you bring to others but His—His perfect, abiding peace. This peace empowers you to walk in victory, overcome life's trials, and become a beacon of hope in a lost and hurting world.

Let today be the day you say yes to His peace.

Let today be the day you step into the fullness of this covenant.

Conclusion

The New Covenant is not just an abstract promise but God's extraordinary invitation to live a life of peace, purpose, and victory in Christ. It's a relationship built on God's faithfulness and sustained by His unmerited grace. This covenant can transform every part of your life, restoring your relationship with God, freeing you from fear, and empowering you to overcome sin.

Embracing the Covenant of Peace is not about striving but resting in Jesus's finished work. When life challenges arise, turn to the One who calms the storms. Be anchored in God's unshakable promises, surrender to Him fully, and allow His truth to shape who you are and how you live.

God's peace is not reserved for perfect moments or perfect people. It's for the weary, the broken, and the struggling—right where you are. Jesus extends His hand through the New Covenant, inviting you to rest in His presence, trust His promises, and step into a life filled with supernatural peace.

But living in this peace requires surrender. It's a daily choice—to trust God above your circumstances, to align your heart with His truth, and to reject the lies that steal your joy. You don't have to earn this peace—you receive it by faith.

The invitation stands. The call is clear. Will you embrace it? Will you say yes? Will you reflect His peace to the world around you? True peace awaits.

Prayer of Surrender and Peace

Jesus, I say yes to Your invitation. I choose to embrace the peace You died to give me. I lay down my striving, my fears, and my need for control. I trust in Your finished work. Teach me to rest in Your presence, to walk in Your truth, and to reflect Your peace to those around me. I receive the gift of Your covenant—Your unshakable love, grace, and victory. Let Your peace rule in my heart, no matter what storms may come. In Jesus' name, Amen.

Three
Discovering My Authority in Christ

When we submit to Jesus' authority, we embrace all He is and everything He has for us. What belongs to Him becomes ours: His righteousness, peace, power, and wisdom. Authority flows from identity, and identity is rooted in submission.

Have you ever felt like you were living below your potential, unsure of your authority in Christ? It's easy to get overwhelmed by the noise of the world and feel powerless or uncertain. But when we submit to Jesus' authority, we access a power that surpasses anything we could achieve.

This authority doesn't come from effort or force; it arises from our identity in Christ—a gift we receive through submitting to His will.

As we embrace all that Jesus represents, we come under His authority. In doing so, we step into all that He has—His righteousness, His peace, His power, and His wisdom. True authority isn't about control; it's about surrendering to Christ. The more we align ourselves with Him, the more His authority flows through us.

Jesus reigns over all realms—heaven, earth, and everything in between. As His followers, we are seated with Him in heavenly places (Ephesians 2:6). Our authority is not limited to earthly matters but extends into the spiritual realm. This divine authority not only transforms how we live; it empowers us to change atmospheres, carry His peace into every situation, and bring His kingdom to earth.

In this chapter, we will explore what it truly means to walk in Christ's authority—not through our own strength but by remaining in Him.

Authority and peace may seem like contrasting concepts, but in God's kingdom, they are intricately intertwined. Romans 16:20a declares: *"And the God of peace will crush Satan under your feet shortly."* This verse reveals that God's peace is not passive—it's a force that actively dismantles chaos and establishes divine order. As followers of Christ, we are called to walk in this type of authority, bringing peace into every sphere of our lives.

Peace Through Authority

To live in peace, we must understand the authority God has given us and use it to govern every part of our lives. True peace doesn't come from merely steering clear of conflict; it arises from submitting to God's authority and allowing His peace to reign within us. The authority to experience peace is rooted in a deep relationship with God. Just as Jesus' authority flowed from His communion with the Father, our authority flows from our connection with Him. Our obedience to God's Word and His Spirit activates this authority to walk in peace.

Authority Rooted in Relationship

A genuine connection with God is essential for understanding and exercising spiritual authority. Without this intimate connection, our efforts to align with His will remain shallow and unsustainable. Spiritual authority is inseparable from relationship. Jesus demonstrated this perfectly in John 5:19, saying: *"Most assuredly, I say to you, the Son can do nothing of Himself, but what He sees the Father do; for whatever He does, the Son also does in like manner."*

He wasn't only following guidelines but living in oneness with the Father. Because of this deep connection, He moved confidently, discerning the Father's will and acting in perfect alignment with Him. In the same way, our authority flows from continuous communion with God.

As we draw closer to God through prayer, worship, and immersion in His Word, our hearts align with His. We begin to discern His will and understand His purposes. In this alignment, we grow in our ability to exercise authority—not by our own strength, but through His. This is why Paul emphasizes in Philippians 2:13: *"For it is God who works in you both to will and to do for His good pleasure."*

God doesn't just call us to obedience—He enables us to desire and carry out His will.

Spiritual authority isn't something we can manufacture or borrow from others; it flows directly from the quality of our relationship with God. Throughout His ministry, Jesus made His dependence on the Father clear. He never acted on His own but only in alignment with the Father's will. This deep connection empowered Him to move in confidence, and the same is true for us—our authority comes from intimacy with God.

Just as Jesus moved confidently because of His deep connection with the Father, we can stand firm when rooted in Him. This connection empowers us to act on His behalf, walking in peace and authority. When our hearts align with God, we are not shaken by challenges or overcome by fear. Instead, we stand secure, knowing who we are in Him and who He is in us. This confidence doesn't stem from self-reliance but from an unshakable trust in God's ability to work through us.

In the same way, our authority must spring from a genuine, intimate relationship with God. Without this, we'll find ourselves powerless, unable to exercise the authority we've been given. Authority without relationship leads to legalism—an empty, rule-based approach to spiritual life that focuses on performance rather than a real connection with God. Jesus rebuked the Pharisees for this in Matthew 23:23, where they followed the law's rules but missed its heart. Our efforts become dry, works-based, and powerless without intimacy with God.

On the other hand, a relationship without authority leads to passivity—knowing God intimately but failing to act on His authority. We see this in the Israelites, who, despite God's promise and presence, shrank back in fear from claiming the land He had promised them. Likewise, a relationship with God without stepping out in His authority leaves us passive, failing to walk in the victory He's already secured for us.

Jesus: The Source of Peace and Authority

Jesus, the Prince of Peace, perfectly demonstrated the union of authority and peace. When He calmed the storm, He rebuked both the wind and the disciples' lack of faith: *"Peace, be still!"* (Mark 4:39)

This moment highlights that peace is not merely a state of inaction but also a command we are called to follow. In John 14:27, Jesus tells us: *"Peace I leave with you, My peace I give to you; not as the world gives do I give to you; let not your heart be troubled, neither let it be afraid."*

This peace is not merely an emotion—it is a divine gift. Like any gift, it requires diligent care and stewardship. To preserve it, we must actively guard our hearts and align ourselves with God's will.

When we surrender our hearts and wills to God, we position ourselves to receive His peace, no matter the challenges that arise. Like Jesus, our peace isn't dependent on external circumstances; it is rooted in our relationship with Him and our authority as His children.

Authority and Trust vs Control

God's authority in our lives isn't about control. It's an invitation to partner with Him. When we truly know God and experience His grace, peace, and faithfulness, obedience stops being a burden and becomes a natural response of love. As Jesus said in John 14:15: *"If you love Me, you will keep My commandments."*

This love is cultivated through prayer, worship, and immersing ourselves in His Word. When we bring Him our fears and failures, He exchanges them for His peace. Trust fuels surrender, and the more we trust Him, the more our desires align with His will.

Paul describes this transformation in Philippians 2:13 (NLT): *"For God is working in you, giving you the desire and the power to do what pleases Him."* As we draw closer to God, He reshapes our desires, aligning them with His and empowering us to walk in His ways.

If you long to walk in God's authority and experience His peace, draw near to Him. Spend time in His presence, listen for His voice, and obey. Trust Him more deeply, depend on Him entirely, and walk in the authority that comes from knowing the One who loves you. This is where true peace is found, and this is where authority begins.

A Picture of Authority

In Matthew 8:5–13, the centurion demonstrates an impressive understanding of authority, revealing a profound truth: true authority comes from being under authority. Accustomed to commanding soldiers and being a man under authority, he recognized Jesus' spiritual dominion and understood that Jesus' words carried divine power. Jesus responded: *"I have not found such great faith, not even in Israel!"* (Matthew 8:10). The centurion's submission to authority empowered him to command with authority.

In the same way, our submission to God's will empowers us to exercise His authority in our lives, bringing peace and divine order into every situation. Just as the centurion's authority came from his submission, our spiritual authority is rooted in surrendering to God's will. When we align ourselves with His Word and His will, we become vessels of His peace, equipping us to overcome fear, turmoil, and conflict.

Submitting Thoughts to God's Authority

One of the most powerful ways to exercise this authority is to take every thought captive and submit it to Jesus' authority. Our minds are often where spiritual battles are fought. When we align our thoughts with God's truth, we stop being influenced by fear, doubt, or lies. Instead, we become empowered by His peace and perspective. As we submit our thoughts to Christ, we begin to operate in greater spiritual authority and stop allowing the enemy's lies to shape our reality.

This submission strengthens our authority over the spiritual realm and allows God's peace to reign in our hearts. As we submit to Him, we begin to walk in a peace that surpasses understanding—a peace that not only guards our hearts but also serves as a testimony of His authority within us. The more we yield to Christ's authority, the more we reflect His power and walk confidently in His entrusted authority.

Authority to Steward Peace

I received back-to-back prophetic words: "You are the homeowner." At first, I thought this meant I was about to get a new physical house. But as I heard it repeatedly, I began to seek clarity from the Holy Spirit. That's when it clicked—God wasn't talking about a house in the natural; He was talking about me.

I am the homeowner. My body, mind, emotions, and soul are the "home" God calls me to steward. I realized I have authority over my thoughts, words, and inner life. Just as I would pray over and protect my physical home, I needed to guard my heart and mind. *"Do you not know that you are the temple of God and that the Spirit of God dwells in you?"* (1 Corinthians 3:16).

This truth became even clearer as I reflected on God's peace. He promises a peace that surpasses understanding (Philippians 4:7), but I had to ask myself: Do I truly believe that peace is mine to experience? The answer was yes. God showed me that the most important place to exercise my authority is within.

Peace is not just a feeling or a passive state; it is a position of authority that requires active stewardship. It is attained by obeying God's voice, submitting to His will, and exercising authority over one's inner world. Peace is the fruit of being filled with the Holy Spirit and walking in His spiritual authority, which begins within.

True peace does not come from controlling external circumstances but from aligning our hearts and minds with God's authority. It is not simply the absence of conflict or struggle; instead, it is the presence of His sovereignty within us, no matter what happens around us. Even in times of trial, we can maintain our peace: *"You will keep in perfect peace*

those whose minds are steadfast because they trust in you"
(Isaiah 26:3, NIV).

When we understand this, peace becomes one of the primary outcomes of our authority, yet it is not the only one. Our authority is not only meant for our own peace; it is intended to bring God's peace, salvation, healing, and deliverance to the world. I can walk in peace because I know under whose authority I stand. I trust that God will guide and protect me. As we carry His peace into a chaotic world, we reflect Jesus, who remained at peace even amid a storm.

Jesus could sleep through the storm because His peace wasn't dependent on His surroundings but on the authority He carried. Likewise, when we walk in God's authority, we don't have to be shaken by external circumstances—we can rest in His perfect peace.

The Authority to Maintain Peace

When we understand our spiritual authority, we recognize that we must actively govern peace. Peace isn't merely the avoidance of conflict; it's the governing presence of God's rule in our lives. Just like a homeowner is responsible for maintaining their property, we are entrusted with keeping our spiritual "home" in order. We cannot allow fear, doubt, or negative thoughts to take residence in our minds and hearts. Our God-given authority empowers us to steward our thoughts and emotions, ensuring they remain aligned with God's truth and peace.

Guarding the Gift of Peace

In Philippians 4:7, we are reminded that God's peace "*surpasses all understanding.*" This peace isn't just a temporary feeling—it is supernatural protection that surrounds our hearts and minds. However, like any valuable gift, it requires careful and intentional attention.

We must actively guard our inner state to preserve peace, much like a homeowner secures their property. This peace is both a gift and a responsibility. To experience it fully, we must remain obedient to God's Word and surrender to His will. When we do, His peace acts as a shield, protecting our hearts and thoughts from anything that might disrupt our inner calm—just as a homeowner locks the doors to protect what belongs inside.

Peace Requires Action

Peace isn't automatic—it requires intentional action. Paul instructs us in 1 Thessalonians 5:16–18: *"Rejoice always, pray without ceasing, in everything give thanks; for this is the will of God in Christ Jesus for you."* Praying, giving thanks, and surrendering our concerns to God are not passive practices—they are acts of spiritual authority. When we trust God and align our thoughts with His truth, we invite His peace to rule our lives.

Activating God's Peace Through His Word

I've experienced this invitation to trust God firsthand. In moments of fear or uncertainty, I've learned to declare God's promises over my circumstances. For example, when fear tries to creep in, I speak 2 Timothy 1:7 aloud: *"For God has not given us a spirit of fear, but of power and of love and of a sound mind."* By speaking these faith-filled words, I activate God's promises, releasing His power to transform my situation. As Isaiah 55:11 reminds us, *"So shall My word be that goes forth from My mouth; it shall not return to Me void, but it shall accomplish what I please, and it shall prosper in the thing for which I sent it."*

When we speak His Word with authority, it accomplishes His purpose in our lives.

A Lesson in Peace: The Cat, the Cows, & the Chaos

One of the clearest lessons I've learned about maintaining peace came from an unexpected situation—a chaotic afternoon involving a cat, some cows, and a whole lot of noise. I found myself overwhelmed by distractions. My neighbor's children raced scooters with blaring sirens, and cows mooed—more like cried out in distress—when I heard a knock at my door. A neighbor informed me that one of our kittens was stuck in a tree and refused to come down.

At that point, I had two choices: try to control and fix the chaos in my own strength or invite Jesus into the situation and exercise my God-given authority. I chose the latter. I paused and asked the Lord how I could partner with Him at this moment. Having been studying authority for this chapter, I knew I needed to take authority over my atmosphere.

I said aloud, "Peace, be still." Immediately, I sensed a shift. Again, I said, "Peace, come and still this chaos." The children stopped racing, the cows returned to the pasture, and even the cat, who I thought was stuck, descended from the tree shortly afterward.

The chaos subsided—not through my efforts alone, but by submitting to Christ's authority and implementing it in my circumstances.

This moment reminded me of a profound truth: peace isn't something we receive passively; it's something we actively manage. We achieve peace by submitting to Jesus's authority in our lives. We maintain peace by aligning ourselves with His will and trusting Him to bring order, even in the most chaotic situations.

True peace is governed by spiritual authority—and that authority is found in Jesus Christ.

Speaking with Authority

Words are more than mere sounds; they are spiritual forces. Proverbs 18:21 says, *"Death and life are in the power of the tongue."* Words can create or destroy, build up or tear down. Jesus demonstrated the authority of words by calming storms, healing the sick, and casting out demons. His words carried divine authority, shaping reality in alignment with the Father's will.

As believers, we are invited to speak with the same authority as Jesus. Faith-filled words activate God's promises, releasing His power to transform circumstances. Jeremiah 1:12 reminds us of God's faithfulness: *"I am watching over My word to perform it."* When we declare His promises, we align our words with Heaven, allowing His authority to shape reality.

I remember a late Saturday afternoon when tension in my marriage had been simmering all day. I found myself at a crossroads: I could react, defend myself, and add fuel to the fire, or I could choose a different path—a path of speaking God's Word with authority to shift the atmosphere.

As I glanced at my husband, I could feel the weight of the situation tightening, as though the tension was reaching a breaking point. Right then, I made a deliberate choice. Instead of responding in frustration, I began to declare the opposite of what I was experiencing.

I spoke words of unity and joy, proclaiming them over our home. I declared the name of Jesus, pleading the blood of Christ over our minds, hearts, and space. I began to pray in tongues, praising God and thanking Him for His peace and presence. I asked the Holy Spirit to guide me, seeking what else I should declare to align with Heaven's truth for our situation. As the words left my mouth, something shifted. The heaviness lifted, and the atmosphere changed. What had been a breeding ground for division transformed into a space where reconciliation and peace could flow. This is how we exercise authority: by replacing lies with truth and declaring God's Word over our lives. Peace is the result of walking in this authority. It's not just an emotional response; it's the fruit of speaking life into our circumstances.

Walking in Authority for Kingdom Peace

Speaking peace is part of walking in our God-given authority. Jesus demonstrated His authority by speaking peace into chaotic situations. When the storm raged, He didn't plead or panic—He commanded, *"Peace, be still!"* (Mark 4:39). Immediately, the wind ceased, and a profound calm settled over the waters.

This moment vividly illustrates the authority we are called to exercise. When chaos threatens to overwhelm us, we don't have to be passive. Like Jesus, we can declare God's peace over our lives and the world around us. He was at peace before the storm, in the storm, and after the storm, modeling the unwavering trust in which we are meant to walk.

Our authority is not about striving or dominating; it's about partnering with God to bring His kingdom to earth. His kingdom is marked by peace: *"For the kingdom of God is not eating and drinking, but righteousness and peace and joy in the Holy Spirit"* (Romans 14:17).

When we walk in our God-given authority, we become carriers of peace. Like Jesus, we can calm storms, heal broken relationships, and bring hope to hopeless situations. This authority isn't based on our strength but on the authority Jesus has given us. As He declared in Matthew 28:18, *"All authority has been given to Me in heaven and on earth."* Because we are His followers, we share in that authority.

I remember the story of the seventy disciples that Jesus sent out in Luke 10. He instructed them to enter the cities and offer peace to those who would receive them. If they were welcomed, they would say, *"Peace to this house,"* but if their peace was not accepted, they would take it back and move on.

When the disciples returned, they were astonished at what they had accomplished in Jesus' name. His instructions were simple yet carried great authority, and He always backs up His Word. That's the beauty of our relationship with Him—just as He empowered them, He empowers us today. As His obedient disciples, we can trust that Jesus backs us up.

Here, Jesus isn't merely suggesting peace—He is revealing its power. He instructs His disciples to release peace over a household, but if they don't receive it, the peace doesn't vanish—it returns to them. This unveils a profound truth: Peace is not just an emotion; it is a spiritual force, an authority we are called to steward, and a gift we have the power to give or reclaim.

Understanding this changes how we walk in authority. So, how do we steward this peace?

In *Take Back Your Authority, Isaac Pitre* [1] powerfully emphasizes that believers are empowered agents of change, not passive bystanders in their spiritual journey. He asserts that many Christians unknowingly surrender their God-given authority, allowing fear, worry, and turmoil to dictate their lives. However, in Christ, we have been given the authority to take back what has been stolen—including our peace.

Pitre encourages believers to recognize their identity as sons and daughters of God, filled with the Holy Spirit, and to actively reclaim their authority to overcome the enemy's attacks and life's challenges. This is not a passive process—it requires intentionality and confidence in the power bestowed upon us through the Holy Spirit. Just as Jesus commanded peace in the midst of the storm, we are called to speak and steward peace in our own lives. By embracing this authority, believers can silence demonic torment, walk in dominion over the works of the enemy, and live in the fullness of God's peace.

Our authority in Christ means that we are not subject to life's storms. We are called to speak peace in every situation, just as Jesus did when He calmed the storm. At that moment, He didn't passively wait for the storm to cease, nor

---

[1]. Pitre, *Take Back Your Authority*

did He hope for it to end. He commanded peace. As believers, we are called to do the same.

It's time to take back our authority. We can no longer allow the enemy, our circumstances, or even our thoughts to rob us of the peace God has promised us. We must actively reclaim our position in Christ, standing firm in the authority He has given us and declaring peace over every situation we face.

Conclusion

Walking in authority is not a distant ideal; it's a daily reality we are called to live out. As the homeowner of your inner world, remember that peace is not just a gift—it's a position. Speak peace, live peace, and steward the authority God has entrusted to you. The storms of life may come, but in Christ, you have the power to calm them. Now is the time to step into this calling—not with fear or hesitation but with faith and boldness, knowing that God is with you and supporting you every step.

Exercising authority and walking in peace is a daily choice—an invitation to live in constant surrender to His will, to trust His guidance, and to allow His peace to reign within your heart and mind. Jesus modeled this life for us and invites us to do the same. When we surrender our fears, align with His will, and declare His promises, we fully step into the authority He has given us.

Now is the time to step into the authority and peace God has given you. Stand firm in His promises and walk boldly in the power entrusted to you. Face each moment with confidence, knowing that in Christ, you have the authority to maintain peace and bring His kingdom to earth.

Invite the Holy Spirit daily, and watch as He transforms fear into faith, doubt into confidence, and struggles into victory.

Four
The Struggle for Holiness

Holiness isn't about striving for perfection or checking items off a religious to-do list. It's not about doing more or trying harder; it's about allowing the Holy Spirit to work in and transform us.

Holiness: A Divine Collaboration

Holiness is a divine collaboration between God and His people—a partnership in which He shapes us to become like Christ. It is not about rigid rules or striving for perfection but about stepping into the fullness of who we were created to be. Psalm 24:3-4 calls us to examine our hearts, ensuring they are clean—free from distractions, idols, and anything that might hinder us from experiencing God's best. This heart posture is essential not only for standing in His holy presence but also for encountering Him fully.

Holiness is not something we achieve through human effort or sheer determination. It is the result of allowing Christ to live in us and through us, yielding our hearts and lives to His transforming work. The Apostle Paul captures this beautifully in Galatians 2:20: *"I have been crucified with Christ; it is no longer I who live, but Christ lives in me; and the life which I now live in the flesh I live by faith in the Son of God, who loved me and gave Himself for me."*

This verse illustrates a profound truth: to live in Christ, we must first die to self. Our old nature must be crucified along with its desires and tendencies so that Christ can fully dwell within us. Paul's words are not just poetry; they are a call to action. Holiness begins with a radical shift in our lives—choosing God's will over our own and trusting in His power to transform us. It is not about striving for perfection or following a set of rules but about allowing God to shape us from the inside out, leading us to excellence.

Holiness is also deeply rooted in relationship

Throughout Scripture, those who walked closely with God reflected His holiness. Moses, for example, experienced such intimacy with God that his face shone after being in His presence. This transformation was not a result of Moses' striving but an outflow of his deep and abiding relationship with God. Likewise, Jesus' disciples, who walked with Him daily, were transformed by His presence. Their lives became marked by His holiness as they drew near to Him.

When crucified with Christ, we align ourselves with His death and resurrection. His victory becomes our victory, and His life becomes our life. This dying-to-self process is not a one-time event but a daily choice—to set aside our will and desires in exchange for His. As we remain in Him, the Holy Spirit empowers us to live a life that reflects His holiness.

Holiness: A Transformation, Not a Burden

Holiness is not a burden; it is a transformation. It is the fruit of abiding in Christ and allowing Him to reshape our thoughts, actions, and character. The more we surrender to Him, the more we begin to experience the fullness of His life within us, and His holiness becomes evident to those around us. Not because we strive to display it but because it flows naturally from a heart yielded to God.

Paul's words remind us that holiness is not about what we can do for God but what He has already done for us. When we live by faith in the Son of God, who loves us and gave Himself for us, we walk in the freedom and joy of His holiness. It is His life in us that makes us holy, and through Him, we can truly live as He directs.

The Battle Starts in Your Mind

Holiness begins in the mind because our thoughts create the foundation for our beliefs, decisions, and actions. How we think influences how we perceive God and respond to His guidance. Our thoughts shape our view of the world around us. What we believe about God, ourselves, and others affects everything. That's why Paul tells us: *"Do not be conformed to this world, but be transformed by the renewing of your mind, that you may prove what is that good and acceptable and perfect will of God"* (Romans 12:2).

I've realized that my thoughts can either bring me closer to God or push me further away from Him. They hold great power. If we don't take them captive, they can create patterns that keep us trapped in negativity. What we focus on expands.

There was a season in my life when negative thoughts quietly ruled my mind. It wasn't loud or dramatic—it was subtle, like background noise I had grown so used to that I didn't even notice it anymore. Little comments would pop into my head: "You're failing," "Things will never change," or "No one really understands you." These thoughts weren't just about me—they began distorting how I saw others. I started seeing situations and people through a negative lens, and I didn't realize how deeply these lies had taken root until they began to spill out of my mouth.

One day, after yet another argument, the Lord convicted my heart. I realized these thoughts weren't just passing moments—they had become my reality—not the ultimate truth, which is Jesus, but the "truth" I was living by. I was seeing my family and circumstances through the lens of my wounds, wounds that I had not fully surrendered to God for healing. These unhealed places wanted a voice, and they had a lot to say.

That realization led me to bring it all to Jesus. I confessed my thoughts, surrendered my pain, and asked Him to replace the lies I had believed with His truth. He reminded me of Philippians 4:8: *"Finally, brethren, whatever things are true, whatever things are noble, whatever things are just, whatever things are pure, whatever things are lovely, whatever things are of good report, if there is any virtue and if there is anything praiseworthy—meditate on these things."*

This verse became my guide for training my mind to think like Jesus. I intentionally aligned my thoughts with God's truth about myself, others, and my circumstances. I started speaking His truth over myself: "*I am loved. I am chosen. I am forgiven.*"

I also prayed, asking God to help me see others through His eyes. Little by little, He replaced my critical thoughts with His perspective—one of love and grace. Slowly, the fog lifted.

Where there had been anger, I responded with kindness. Where there had been turmoil, I discovered peace.

When our hearts and minds align with Jesus, we see situations and people through His eyes. Instead of dwelling on frustrations or failures, we can focus on what is good, lovely, and true. This doesn't mean ignoring the pain or pretending negativity doesn't exist—it means bringing it to the One who can transform it.

Holiness begins here, in the renewal of the mind. As God aligns our thoughts with His truth, He empowers us to walk in purity, peace, and purpose. The lesson I've learned is one I carry with me every day:

- I can't have a thought about anyone, including myself, that God doesn't have.

- God's thoughts are always rooted in love and truth.

Aligning Your Thoughts with God's Truth

When a thought lingers long enough, it begins to feel like truth—even if it's a lie. These lies can hold us back from hearing God or experiencing His peace. Our thoughts act like magnets; what we think or believe starts to manifest in our lives. This is why we must renew our minds and cleanse our hearts, trading our version of truth for His absolute truth.

Here's the key: God's truth isn't just an idea; it's a person, Jesus. When we renew our minds with the Word, it changes how we think, how we feel, and eventually, how we live. Romans 8:6 says: *"For to be carnally minded is death; but to be spiritually minded is life and peace."*

The Holy Spirit guides us in aligning our thoughts with the life and peace found in Jesus. I have also noticed that during these moments, it can feel as if we are double-minded when our minds and hearts are out of sync. This often stems from a wounded heart. While the mind operates on logic and reason, the heart is shaped by emotions and past experiences. Scripture tells us that a double-minded person is unstable in all their ways. (James 1:8)

Guarding Your Heart and Mind

Proverbs 4:23 instructs: *"Keep your heart with all diligence, for out of it spring the issues of life."* But guarding our hearts also means guarding our minds—some would even say they are one and the same. When we allow negative or toxic thoughts to linger, they can act like filters, distorting how we see God, hear Him, and live out His will.

I've experienced this firsthand. There have been times when I didn't realize I had a "dirty filter" in my thinking until God lovingly revealed it to me.

There was a specific moment when God revealed a mindset I hadn't even realized I had—a hidden belief that was quietly shaping my reactions and choices. This happened during a conversation with someone I deeply cared about. I don't remember exactly what they said, but I felt myself reacting defensively, almost aggressively, trying to control the situation. As soon as the words left my mouth, I knew something deeper was going on.

I later sat with that moment and asked God, *"Why did I act that way? What is at the root of this response?"* As I prayed, God gently revealed to me that my reaction came from a place of self-protection—an instinctive behavior I had developed as a child to navigate an unsafe and unpredictable world. In those moments of uncertainty or fear, I learned to control situations, often through manipulation, defensiveness, or even aggression, to regain a sense of power and security.

God revealed that although those behaviors may have been survival mechanisms in my younger years, they no longer served me and certainly weren't aligned with His heart for my life. In fact, they were holding me back from experiencing the freedom and peace He intended for me.

He brought me to Proverbs 3:5-6: *"Trust in the Lord with all your heart and lean not on your own understanding; in all your ways acknowledge Him, and He shall direct your paths."*

I realized my reactions were rooted in a lack of trust in Him. I was trying to take control because, deep down, I didn't fully believe that God would protect me, guide me, or work things out for good.

It was humbling to admit that my self-protective behaviors were a sign of misplaced faith. I had been relying on myself rather than surrendering to Him. But in His kindness, God didn't just show me the problem; He also showed me the solution. He began teaching me how to exchange my old reactions for His truth.

When I felt the urge to control or manipulate, I paused to pray instead, asking Him, "What is the truth in this situation? How do you want me to respond?" The more I practiced this, the more I noticed a shift in my heart and relationships. The need for control lessened as I learned to lean into God's promises. I began responding to others with more grace and patience because I wasn't carrying the burden of trying to manage everything myself.

This journey has profoundly transformed my relationship with God. By learning to trust Him more deeply, I have witnessed how His Word and ways foster peace and healing within my heart and in my interactions with others. While it is an ongoing process, it continually draws me closer to Him.

The Role of Holiness and Character Development

For the peace of the Holy Spirit to flow freely in our lives, we must pursue holiness. A pure vessel, free from bitterness or sin, allows God's power to move freely. Pursuing holiness isn't about perfection but about submission—allowing the Holy Spirit to purify us from within and lead us into godliness. As we mature spiritually, we become more sensitive to His voice, more willing to obey, and more aligned with His will. 1 Peter 1:16 reminds us: *"Because it is written, 'Be holy, for I am holy."*

Holiness and character development are essential to walking in the fullness of God's power. The Holy Spirit transforms us to reflect Christ's nature, cultivating the fruit of the Spirit—love, joy, peace, patience, kindness, goodness, faithfulness, gentleness, and self-control (Galatians 5:22). This transformation is ongoing and requires a constant yielding to His work within us.

When we yield to the transformative power of the Holy Spirit, our character aligns with Christ's nature. Our hearts are healed, cleansed, and made whole. The fruit of the Spirit begins to overflow naturally, impacting those around us—not through our own efforts but because of His presence within us.

Our character must match the calling God has placed on our lives. The Holy Spirit will not pour His power into a vessel unprepared to carry it. As we reflect Christ's character, we experience His peace more deeply, both internally and in our relationships. This peace empowers us to live confidently, fulfilling the divine purpose for which we were created.

Holiness and Peace Go Hand in Hand

Holiness isn't just about following a set of rules or performing rituals; it's about living in harmony with God's heart. It's a continuous journey of aligning ourselves with His will and allowing His peace to flow through every part of our lives. As we pursue holiness, we are drawn into a deeper intimacy with Him, and His peace becomes a constant companion. Jesus declared: *"Peace I leave with you, my peace I give unto you: not as the world giveth, give I unto you. Let not your heart be troubled, neither let it be afraid"* (John 14:27).

His peace isn't just a momentary feeling; it's the fruit of walking closely with Him. As we align our hearts with God's truth, we create space for His peace to dwell in us. Holiness doesn't just bring peace; it forms a protective barrier that shields us from life's storms. Like a house built on a firm foundation, His peace keeps us steady, unshaken, and unmoved.

Peace is more than just an emotion; it is a state of being that flows from the presence of the Holy Spirit. To truly experience this peace, we must live in His power and submit to His guidance each day. As we cultivate a deeper relationship with Him, we grow in trust, allowing His presence to fill us with a peace that surpasses all understanding.

In this divine partnership, holiness and peace are intertwined. The more we align with God's will, the more His peace fills our hearts, guards us in every season, and keeps us anchored in His love.

Holiness: A Journey of Renewal and Alignment

Holiness is not a checklist of actions or an outward performance to be measured. It's not about striving to meet external standards or following rituals without a heart of purpose. Holiness isn't about trying to prove we're "good enough" through our own effort or putting on a facade for others. Instead, it's deeply rooted in a relationship with God, marked by inner transformation. Holiness is the result of surrendering fully to God's work in us—aligning our hearts and actions with His will through His power, not our own. Jesus' invitation to this divine exchange is clear:

"Abide in Me, and I in you. As the branch cannot bear fruit of itself unless it abides in the vine, neither can you unless you abide in Me. I am the vine; you are the branches. He who abides in Me, and I in him, bears much fruit; for without Me, you can do nothing" (John 15:4-5).

Our relationship with the Holy Spirit embodies a divine synergy. He dwells within us, and we abide in Him. Just as a branch depends on the vine for nourishment, we rely on Christ for everything. This mutual indwelling transforms and empowers us to live victoriously. As we remain in Christ, His life flows through us, producing fruit that reflects His love, peace, and power. We no longer rely on our own strength but are continually renewed and aligned with His divine purposes.

This constant connection with Christ is the source of our strength and peace, even during life's most challenging seasons. Peace flows naturally from abiding in Him as we rest in His sufficiency and allow the Spirit to guide us. Through this ongoing, life-giving relationship, we are empowered to walk in faith, love, and authority, revealing His presence and power to the world around us. The fruit we bear in alignment with His will serves as evidence of His work in us, testifying to His transforming power.

A Mindset Transformed by Holiness

The greatest battles for holiness aren't first fought through our actions; they are won or lost in our minds. Every thought leads us either toward God's truth or away from it. How we think shapes how we live, and without a renewed mind, true holiness remains out of reach. Romans 12:2 encourages us to be transformed by the renewing of our minds. This renewal allows us to discern God's perfect will, providing clarity and direction in our lives.

I remember a season when I felt completely overwhelmed by the weight of responsibility in my life. I was juggling family, ministry, and personal struggles, and it seemed like no matter how much effort I put in, it was never enough. My thoughts were a constant swirl of self-doubt and anxiety, whispering, "You're going to fail. You can't do this. Why even try?"

One day, after another sleepless night, I broke down in prayer, pouring out my feelings of inadequacy. In that vulnerable moment, I sensed God prompting me to open His Word. Reluctantly, I opened my Bible, and my eyes landed on 2 Corinthians 12:9: *"My grace is sufficient for you, for My strength is made perfect in weakness."*

It felt like a floodlight had been turned on in the darkness of my mind. God wasn't inviting me to be enough in my own strength; He was asking me to rely on His. Slowly, I began replacing the lies I had been listening to with the truth of Scripture. I meditated on Romans 8:37: *"Yet in all these things we are more than conquerors through Him who loved us."* I spoke Philippians 4:13 over myself: *"I can do all things through Christ who strengthens me."*

As I renewed my mind with His Word, the confusion and anxiety began to lift. It didn't happen overnight, but each time those old lies crept back in, I fought them with the truth. I declared what God said about me, not what I felt. Over time, peace replaced the chaos in my mind.

That season taught me that my thoughts, left unchecked, could lead me down a path of despair. But it also taught me that winning the battle in my mind was just the first step—true transformation came when I consistently aligned my thoughts with God's truth. Now, whenever I feel overwhelmed, I check my thoughts—if they don't align with God's Word, I know they need to be renewed again.

Holiness is more than a moment of surrender; it's a daily process of choosing God's truth over the enemy's lies. If I have a thought about myself that God doesn't have, I know it's not from Him. And if I don't take authority over my thoughts, they will take authority over me.

The Cycle of Thoughts, Feelings, and Actions

Ford Taylor's Thoughts, Feelings, Actions [1] *(TFA)* model shows how the cycle begins with our thoughts. What we think about—whether it's grounded in truth or not—stirs up emotions, and those emotions influence our actions. Over time, these actions form habits that shape our behavior, and our behavior ultimately defines our character.

When we repeatedly meditate on specific thoughts, whether true or false, they generate feelings that influence our decisions. If we fail to align our thoughts with God's truth, they can distort our perception of reality. These distorted thoughts can become "our truth," shaping how we view the world. This is why we must take our thoughts captive (2 Corinthians 10:5) and filter them through God's word, or else they risk becoming a lie we believe.

---

1. Taylor, *Relactional Leadership.*

The ultimate truth is Jesus Christ (John 14:6). When we align our thinking with Him, we experience the transformative power of holiness. A mind renewed in Christ and aligned with God's Word brings clarity to hear God's voice, discern His will, and walk in His peace. Romans 8:6 reminds us that the carnal mind leads to death, but a spiritual mind brings life and peace. By aligning our thoughts with God's truth, we not only foster holiness but also unlock the fullness of His shalom—a state of wholeness, freedom, and rest.

I recall being defensive and accusatory during a conflict with a close friend. I felt wronged and was quick to believe the worst in them. Those negative thoughts festered and led to resentment. I began avoiding them instead of seeking a resolution, letting the distance grow. The more I allowed those thoughts to linger, the more my actions reflected them—coldness, distance, and an unwillingness to reach out. I wasn't acting like the person I wanted to be, and I knew something needed to change.

One day, I felt God gently convict me, reminding me of 2 Corinthians 10:5: *"We are destroying speculations and every lofty thing raised up against the knowledge of God, and we are taking every thought captive to the obedience of Christ."*

I realized my thoughts had been controlling me, fueling the conflict, and causing a wall between us. I needed to take those thoughts captive—not just the situation but the lies I had believed about my friend and myself.

So, I prayed and asked God to show me His truth. Instead of dwelling on my hurt, I began to meditate on verses like Ephesians 4:31-32, which reminded me to put away bitterness and be kind and forgiving. I asked God for His perspective on the situation, and He helped me see my friend's actions through a lens of compassion, not offense.

Something shifted within me as I surrendered my thoughts and replaced them with God's truth. The breakthrough came when I chose to align my thoughts with God's Word, allowing peace to replace the tension and letting forgiveness flow where bitterness once resided. My heart softened, and I approached my friend with humility, ready to reconcile.

But the change didn't stop with me. As I approached my friend with an open heart—feeling vulnerable and eager to restore our relationship—I noticed the atmosphere between us shift as well. It wasn't immediate, but as I allowed God's peace to reign in my heart, it started to touch my friend's heart, too. The tension that once lingered began to fade. Over time, we resolved our differences—not because of a perfect conversation or a sudden change in circumstances but because I chose to align my thoughts with God's truth, allowing His peace to transform my responses.

That incident taught me the power of taking every thought captive and surrendering it to God. By doing so, I broke free from the cycle of negativity and opened the door for healing and restoration in our relationship. Holiness isn't just about personal peace; it's about how it spills over into every area of our lives, transforming not only our hearts but the hearts of those around us.

The heart and mind are deeply interconnected. Our thoughts shape our emotions; over time, what we dwell on in our minds settles into our hearts. This is why Scripture emphasizes not only taking thoughts captive but also diligently guarding our hearts: *"Keep your heart with all diligence, for out of it spring the issues of life"* (Proverbs 4:23).

When left unchecked, our thoughts and beliefs become filters that distort how we hear God and discern His will. Holiness demands vigilance—uprooting lies, renewing our minds, and aligning our hearts with God's truth.

Living by the Spirit, Not the Flesh

Paul contrasts living by the flesh with living by the Spirit in Romans 8:5-6: *"For those who live according to the flesh set their minds on the things of the flesh, but those who live according to the Spirit, the things of the Spirit. For to be carnally minded is death, but to be spiritually minded is life and peace."*

To walk in the peace of the Spirit, we must choose to die to the desires of the flesh and yield to the guidance of the Holy Spirit. This cannot be achieved through willpower alone; it requires the Spirit's power to free us from distractions and align us with God's will.

Living by the Spirit involves a conscious act of surrender. Our natural tendencies—pride, envy, and division—draw us toward the flesh, but the Spirit guides us into peace, love, and unity. The more we yield to the Holy Spirit, the more we experience the transformative power. As we submit ourselves to Him, we align our hearts and minds with His will, allowing His peace to take root in us.

Holiness requires both stillness and action. In stillness, we quiet our minds to recognize God's presence, allowing His truth to shape us. In action, we move forward in obedience, partnering with Heaven to fulfill His purposes. Walking in holiness involves not only receiving revelation but also stepping out in obedience. When we move in obedience, miracles happen, and heaven meets earth.

One of the most beautiful aspects of living by the Spirit is that His peace flows naturally through us. When we allow the Holy Spirit to reign in us, His peace is not just a passing emotion—it becomes a constant presence, shaping how we live and interact with the world around us. This peace guards our hearts and minds, enabling us to live out our divine calling with confidence and joy.

As we continue to yield to the Spirit, we find freedom from the distractions and chaos of our flesh. We are no longer driven by selfish desires or the struggle to manage our emotions. Instead, we walk in peace, love, and power, reflecting God's heart in everything we do. Living by the Spirit empowers us to face trials with courage, to walk boldly in our purpose, and to experience God's supernatural peace in every situation.

Surrender and Trust in Holiness

Surrender isn't just sitting back; it's a courageous, active choice to place our trust in God's perfect wisdom and loving nature. It's opening our hearts to the One who understands us better than we understand ourselves, and in that trust, we find our deepest freedom.

Psalm 139:1-3 says: *"O Lord, You have searched me and known me. You know my sitting down and my rising up; You understand my thought afar off. You comprehend my path and my lying down and are acquainted with all my ways."*

These verses remind us that God's knowledge of us is complete and unwavering. He understands every detail of our lives—our struggles, our desires, our weaknesses—and He holds them with perfect love and holiness.

If God knows us this deeply and loves us so completely, why would we ever withhold our trust from Him? Surrendering to His holiness isn't about losing ourselves but rather about gaining the fullness of who He created us to be. When we yield to His holiness, we embrace a path of divine peace and unwavering security. In His holiness, we are both fully known and fully loved—perfectly safe in His presence.

The more we surrender, the more we align ourselves with the truth of who He is and who He has created us to be. Ask the Holy Spirit to reveal areas in your life where you may still be holding onto control, where your trust may be wavering. What steps can you take today to fully surrender those areas to God, allowing His holiness to fill you with peace and rest?

Overcoming Barriers to Holiness

Even as we surrender, obstacles often hinder our connection with God and His holiness. These barriers can take the form of magnified fears, destructive thought patterns, or overwhelming emotions that demand our focus. When we give these voices more attention than God's truth, we feel distant, confused, and stuck.

But God has given us tools to overcome these barriers. Worship and gratitude recalibrate our focus. They shift our minds away from our circumstances and back to God's character, power, and presence. Philippians 4:6-7 says: *"Be anxious for nothing, but in everything by prayer and supplication, with thanksgiving, let your requests be made known to God; and the peace of God, which surpasses all understanding, will guard your hearts and minds through Christ Jesus."*

When fear or chaos clouds your vision, stop and worship. Declare who God is and offer gratitude for what He has done and is still doing. Worship lifts us above the noise, helping us see from heaven's perspective. Holiness thrives when we guard our hearts and align our focus with His truth.

Ask yourself:

- What wrong voices or fears have I allowed to take center stage?

- How can I use worship and gratitude today to shift my perspective?

Walking in the Spirit

Walking in the Spirit requires yielding, surrendering control, and trusting God completely. Romans 12:1-2 urges us: *"I beseech you therefore, brethren, by the mercies of God, that you present your bodies a living sacrifice, holy, acceptable to God, which is your reasonable service. And do not be conformed to this world, but be transformed by the renewing of your mind, that you may prove what is that good and acceptable and perfect will of God."*

This process of yielding connects directly to the call in Romans 12:1 to offer ourselves as living sacrifices. Our flesh cannot overcome sin through willpower alone—true transformation occurs only through the power of the Holy Spirit. As we allow the Spirit to guide, shape, and empower us, we are progressively transformed into Christ's likeness. This transformation is not a one-time event but a continual process of surrender and renewal.

When we train ourselves to follow the Spirit's leading, the power of our sinful nature loses its grip. Galatians 5:16 reminds us: *"I say then: Walk in the Spirit, and you shall not fulfill the lust of the flesh."* The peace of the Spirit often serves as confirmation, guiding us along the right path and offering assurance, even during uncertainty.

When we surrender to God's work in us, we do not just let go of control; we actively choose to yield to the Holy Spirit's guidance in every moment. The Spirit gives us the strength to resist the pull of the flesh and experience the freedom that comes with living in holiness. This daily act of surrender transforms us more fully into Christ's image, enabling us to walk in the peace and purpose that God has designed for us.

Embracing Holiness

Holiness begins with a choice—surrender. It's about letting go of control, our plans, and our ways and fully trusting God to guide our steps. Surrender is not just about relinquishing control over circumstances; it's about submitting ourselves to God's process. When I surrendered my desire to control my marriage, I witnessed a profound shift—not in my husband's actions but in my own heart. I found healing, patience, and a renewed perspective. Through this surrender, God worked in me, transforming my heart and allowing me to reflect His holiness in my marriage.

Through Christ, we reflect God's glory, walking in His peace and power. I can't even begin to describe how much pursuing holiness has transformed my marriage. Looking back, externally, nothing seemed to change—my husband remained the same, still facing his own struggles—but everything within me shifted. This didn't happen overnight. Only after intentionally renewing my mind and healing from past hurts did I realize that the way I saw him, reacted, and handled our relationship had been completely transformed.

There was a time when our relationship was filled with conflict, defensiveness, and a constant battle for who was right or who had more authority. We would argue just to be heard, to prove our point, and often strive to control the situation—all rooted in fear. Fear of being misunderstood, fear of rejection, fear of feeling powerless. But as God began working on my heart, as I pursued holiness and aligned myself more closely with His character, everything inside me started to change.

I realized that holiness isn't just about following rules or living perfectly; it's about allowing God to heal my heart and refine my reactions. As He healed me, I started to approach my marriage differently. No longer did I feel the need to control or prove myself. Instead, I began to rest in the truth that I am enough because of Christ and that my husband's actions or words no longer define my worth.

The breakthrough came when I stood on the promise in 1 Corinthians 7:14: *"The wife sanctifies the unbelieving husband."* While my husband is a believer, I hold tightly to the truth of this verse, knowing that our oneness in Christ can bring transformation to both our hearts, regardless of where each of us is in our journey. I believe that my pursuit of holiness, my submission to God, and my willingness to allow God to work in me can impact both of us. Even though the change started in me, I trust that as I grow in Christ, it will bring transformation to our marriage and to both of our hearts. I claimed that promise, knowing that God's work in me has the power to sanctify us both.

And you know what happened? An incredible peace and joy settled into our marriage. I no longer feel anxious about whether he will change or whether he will understand my perspective. I feel an unwavering peace, knowing that God is actively working in both of us—healing our hearts and sanctifying our marriage, shaping us into the people He destined us to be. This peace isn't dependent on how my husband responds. It comes from the peace I've found in pursuing holiness. His actions no longer shake me. I am free to love and support him—regardless of his journey—because my peace flows from God, not from circumstances. It's a beautiful place of surrender and trust, knowing that God is faithful to complete the work He has started in us.

This pursuit of holiness has transformed our marriage—not because it changed the circumstances, but because it changed me. When my heart was healed, it brought healing to our relationship. I believe that when we surrender to God and pursue holiness, He does a transformative work in us that radiates to everyone around us, especially in our marriages. This testimony is part of my journey, and I know that the peace and joy I experience today can be a reality for anyone who chooses to surrender to God and walk in the peace that comes from holiness

Conclusion: Embracing Holiness

This journey of aligning my thoughts and actions with God's truth has been life-changing—not just for me but also for the relationships around me. As I surrendered my thoughts, feelings, and actions to God, He replaced bitterness with compassion and resentment with peace. The process wasn't always quick or easy, but it was through surrendering to God's process that my heart was healed and my relationships restored.

Holiness not only changes our hearts but also transforms everything around us. It reshapes our relationships, deepens our understanding of love, and fosters a peace that endures beyond circumstances. As we surrender, trust, and walk in the Spirit, we reflect God's peace more fully.

It is the divine synergy of His life in us and our life in Him, a sacred union where His power renews and strengthens us. This mystery transforms and empowers us to reflect His glory. As we persevere in renewing our minds and guarding our hearts, we will walk in the fullness of His peace and purpose, shining as lights in a world that desperately needs His truth.

Holiness isn't just about personal peace; it's about the peace that overflows into every corner of our lives, touching others and transforming relationships. When we allow God to renew our minds and take every thought captive, we can break free from destructive thought patterns—fear, doubt, and frustration—that so often control us. As we surrender to Him, His peace doesn't remain confined within us; it becomes a force that brings healing, restoration, and reconciliation to the relationships around us.

In the end, the peace we seek is not just for our own well-being but for the world around us. We are called to be living testimonies of God's grace and restorative power. Through our actions, words, and relationships, we extend His peace to others. As we walk in holiness, we become instruments of His peace—receiving and sharing it with the desperate world.

Five

Walking in Peace, Empowered by the Spirit

"I say then: Walk in the Spirit, and you shall not
fulfill the lust of the flesh." Galatians 5:1

Praying in the Spirit: Unlocking Peace and Power

In previous chapters, we've explored foundational truths
such as living in surrender, walking in holiness, and relying
on the guidance of the Holy Spirit. Now, we are called to
put these principles into practice. This chapter focuses on
praying in the Spirit—a practice that deepens our connec-

tion with God's presence and empowers us to walk in His peace. Inspired by Dave Roberson's The Walk of the Spirit, The Walk of Power, we recognize that peace is not just a byproduct of the Spirit but an essential thread woven into our relationship with Him.

Praying, Growing, Becoming

Praying in the Spirit is more than a spiritual exercise—it's a daily practice that requires faith, intentionality, and commitment. As we yield to the Spirit's direction and cultivate a Spirit-led mindset, we experience transformation from the inside out. This sacred form of communication strengthens and empowers us, inviting God's peace to permeate every area of our lives.

One of the most powerful gifts the Holy Spirit gives for spiritual growth and peace is praying in tongues for personal edification. As Roberson explains in his book, praying in the Spirit bypasses the limitations of our natural understanding, enabling us to connect with God on a supernatural level. Though the world may see it as unnecessary, it is a divine gift that builds our faith and brings clarity where human reasoning falls short.

When we pray in the Spirit—whether through speaking in tongues or simply following the Spirit's promptings—we strengthen our inner man, align ourselves with God's divine plan, and increase our capacity to fulfill our calling

Praying in Tongues Unlocks the Supernatural

Praying in tongues is a supernatural language given by the Holy Spirit, enabling believers to communicate beyond their human understanding. This powerful form of prayer transforms the atmosphere around us—both internally and externally—bringing the peace of God that surpasses understanding into our emotions, environment, and life circumstances.

Paul emphasized its value when he said: *"I thank my God I speak with tongues more than you all"* (1 Corinthians 14:18), showing how integral this practice was to his spiritual life. When we pray in tongues, we speak mysteries revealed by the Spirit (1 Corinthians 14:2), bypassing our intellect and emotions so that God's wisdom and revelation can flow freely into our lives. As Romans 8:26 declares: *"The Spirit Himself makes intercession for us with groanings which cannot be uttered."* As Roberson explains, praying in tongues builds our spiritual foundation, making us more receptive to revelation knowledge and the leading of the Spirit.

The more we engage in this practice, the stronger our spirit becomes as we build ourselves up on our most holy faith (Jude 1:20). This supernatural language is both a weapon and a tool, empowering us to release God's intentions in our lives. The Holy Spirit not only strengthens our spirits but also renews our character, helping us become more attuned to His voice and leading.

Living a Spirit-Led Life

The Holy Spirit is not only our Comforter but also our Guide, leading us into a deeper walk with God. Living in His power is not a one-time event but a continual journey of surrender, growth, and partnership. Jesus assured us in John 14:26: *"But the Helper, the Holy Spirit, whom the Father will send in My name, He will teach you all things and bring to your remembrance all things that I said to you."*

While we will explore surrender in depth in a later chapter, it is essential to recognize how it connects to our prayer life and relationship with the Holy Spirit. When we pray in tongues, we surrender our natural reasoning and allow the Holy Spirit to pray through us. This act of faith opens the door to divine encounters, supernatural peace, and God's perfect guidance.

I remember a time when I was overwhelmed by uncertainty. It felt as though I was drowning in fear. But as I surrendered those emotions to the Holy Spirit and prayed in tongues, His peace washed over me. He reminded me of Romans 8:6: *"For to be carnally minded is death, but to be spiritually minded is life and peace."* At that moment, the Spirit reoriented my focus toward Jesus, anchoring me in His truth. When we lean on our own understanding, we limit what God can do, but when we surrender to His leading, we receive clarity, wisdom, and peace that cannot be shaken by circumstances.

What I love most about the Holy Spirit is how He continually reveals Jesus to us. Just as Jesus reveals the Father, the Spirit testifies of Christ. *"When the Helper comes... He will testify of Me"* (John 15:26). The more we yield to Him, the more we see Jesus in His fullness—His love, mercy, and power. This is the key to a Spirit-filled life: walking in divine revelation and allowing God's peace to anchor us.

As we surrender to the Holy Spirit in prayer, we invite His presence to lead every area of our lives—from decision-making to relationships and overcoming trials. He empowers us to rise above challenges, persevere in faith, and remain rooted in God's peace. Romans 8:14 reminds us: *"For as many as are led by the Spirit of God, these are sons of God."*

A Spirit-led life is one of continual surrender, where we lean not on our own understanding but trust in His divine wisdom. As we yield to Him, we receive clarity, peace, and strength beyond our natural ability. This is the power of walking in the Spirit—living fully aligned with God's will, anchored in His presence, and transformed by His truth.

Revelation Knowledge Through the Spirit

Praying in tongues and living in the Spirit unlocks revelation and insight that surpasses human understanding. The Holy Spirit is our teacher, unveiling the mysteries of God's Word and empowering us to grasp truths that would otherwise remain hidden. This revelation strengthens our faith and equips us to walk in the fullness of God's power and purpose.

Praying in tongues unlocks spiritual understanding. When we pray in the Spirit, the Holy Spirit imparts wisdom and insight beyond our natural comprehension. As 1 Corinthians 2:10 declares: *"But God has revealed them to us through His Spirit. For the Spirit searches all things, yes, the deep things of God."* In these moments of Spirit-led prayer, we move beyond the limitations of our human intellect and tap into the mind of Christ, receiving divine strategies, direction, and understanding. This supernatural insight enables us to walk with confidence, knowing that God is guiding us according to His perfect will.

As I deepened my practice of praying in tongues, my mind was renewed, and my perspective shifted. There were moments of clarity and revelation that I could not attribute to my own reasoning. In times of confusion or uncertainty, the Holy Spirit would illuminate scriptures I had read before but had not fully understood. Through this practice, I realized that praying in the Spirit is like opening a direct line of divine revelation from God's heart to ours.

Romans 8:28 reminds us that all things work together for our good because we are called according to God's purpose. The Holy Spirit is actively working on our behalf, aligning our lives with God's divine plan. Through our prayers in the Spirit, He replaces any plan or thought that is contrary to God's will, aligning us with His perfect purpose. We do not need to rely on our own understanding or the wisdom of the world to discern God's will. As John 16:13 affirms: *"However, when He, the Spirit of truth, has come, He will guide you into all truth."*

As we pray in tongues, we align ourselves more closely with God's heart, tapping into a well of wisdom and revelation that can only be accessed through the Holy Spirit. This intimacy with the Spirit not only reveals divine truths but also provides the peace that surpasses all understanding (Philippians 4:7). The more we yield to the Spirit's leading, the more we begin to think with the mind of Christ and see with His perspective. This peace becomes an anchor in life's challenges, grounding our hearts and minds with clarity and assurance.

This is the power of praying in the Spirit—gaining access to God's mind, receiving revelation, and experiencing a peace that confirms His will. It is an invitation to deeper intimacy with God—to walk by faith, not by sight, and to step boldly into the fullness of His plans.

Intercession: Partnering with the Holy Spirit

The Holy Spirit leads us into intercession, empowering us to stand in the gap for others according to God's will. Whether we are praying for a family member, friend, or nation, Spirit-led intercession becomes a divine catalyst for breakthrough.

Standing in the gap with Jesus, under the direction of the Holy Spirit, is an act of love in action. We trust that as our prayers align with God's will, He will move powerfully to bring about transformation. Through intercession, we invite the Holy Spirit into every situation, giving Him full authority to work. This form of prayer is not only a blessing to others—it strengthens our own faith and aligns us with God's purposes.

Intercession is also a form of spiritual warfare. As we pray in tongues, we engage in battle against the forces of darkness that seek to hinder God's will. Yet, even in spiritual warfare, we experience peace, knowing that God is fighting on our behalf.

1 Peter 3:11–12 reminds us: *"Let him turn away from evil and do good; let him seek peace and pursue it. For the eyes of the Lord are on the righteous, and His ears are open to their prayers."* This verse assures us that God hears us when we intercede. Through the power of the Holy Spirit, our prayers break strongholds, push back darkness, and bring lasting transformation.

Interceding in tongues is a supernatural tool that releases God's will on earth. As we pray in the Spirit, we participate in establishing His Kingdom, fulfilling Jesus' words: *"Your kingdom come, Your will be done on earth as it is in heaven"* (Matthew 6:10).

Conclusion: Walking in the Power of the Spirit

Living in constant connection with the Holy Spirit is essential for walking in the fullness of God's plan. The Spirit is our teacher, guide, and source of peace. He leads us into all truth and aligns us with God's perfect will. As we yield to Him—through prayer, obedience, and intimacy—we step into supernatural wisdom, strength, and divine peace beyond human understanding.

Praying in tongues is one of the most powerful ways to cultivate this connection. This practice strengthens our spirit and anchors us in God's unshakable peace. When life's trials arise, praying in the Spirit empowers us to navigate them with bold faith, clarity, and confidence in God's perfect will.

Walking in the Spirit means experiencing freedom, boldness, and supernatural empowerment. Through Him, we gain divine strategies and unwavering peace. We are never alone—the Holy Spirit is our constant companion, guiding us with wisdom and filling us with peace that surpasses all understanding (Philippians 4:7).

As you surrender to the Spirit's leading, His peace will transform every area of your life. This peace is not fleeting; it is eternal and deeply rooted in God's presence. It enables you to walk boldly in your purpose, face trials with courage, and live with unwavering faith.

By living in the power of the Holy Spirit, you embrace a life of peace, strength, and divine fulfillment—grounded in His presence and empowered by His might

Six

Awakening Our True Purpose

Living in the Spirit awakens our true purpose. When the soul is surrendered to the Spirit, we step into the peace and power designed for our divine calling.

Living in the Spirit: Discovering True Purpose

Living in the Spirit is not simply about following rules or chasing blessings. It is about awakening our spirits to their true purpose: intimate fellowship with God. This fellowship anchors us in His peace and guides us through every moment. But living in the Spirit is not a one-time decision; it's a daily choice to surrender our understanding and align every part of our lives with His will. Through this continual surrender, we experience true transformation and step into the fullness of our identity as children of God, empowered by His Spirit.

Understanding Nephesh: The Living Soul

The original Hebrew word for soul, *nephesh*, refers to more than just the mind, will, and emotions. It represents the whole person—their life, breath, desires, and entire being. Nephesh serves as the bridge between the physical and spiritual realms, uniting mind, body, and spirit as one.

While the soul encompasses our mind, will, and emotions, it was never meant to take the lead. When it takes control, confusion and unrest follow. The spirit—the eternal part of us—is where the Holy Spirit dwells, allowing us to hear God's voice and receive His guidance. When the spirit leads and the soul submits, divine order is restored, bringing forth God's peace.

Hebrews 4:12 illustrates the distinction between soul and spirit: *"For the word of God is living and powerful, and sharper than any two-edged sword, piercing even to the division of soul and spirit, and of joints and marrow, and is a discerner of the thoughts and intents of the heart."*

Just as joints and marrow are intertwined yet distinct, so are the soul and spirit—deeply connected but not the same.

Recognizing this distinction is key to walking in alignment with God.

Training the Soul to Walk in Peace

Aligning our inner life with the Holy Spirit's guidance is a daily practice. It requires pausing when emotions surge, seeking His perspective before we react, and allowing the Word of God to show us where our soul has taken control instead of our spirit. As we invite Him to realign us, clarity, stability, and deep peace follow.

The soul—our inner self shaped by experiences, desires, and thoughts—is meant to respond to the spirit, which communicates with God. When we let reasoning dictate our decisions, we feel instability and a disconnection from His presence. However, when the spirit guides us, we are anchored in God's peace, clarity, and purpose, no longer swayed by external circumstances but firmly rooted in Him.

This is why training the soul is vital. A soul that learns to yield to the spirit no longer reacts out of fear or circumstance but operates from a place of trust in God's leadership. This shift positions us to walk in the fullness of His power, peace, and joy.

Aligning Soul and Spirit: The Way to Peace

To live a Spirit-led life, we must intentionally train our souls to submit to the guidance of the Holy Spirit. This training is foundational to experiencing peace, as it brings order to the inner conflict between our will and God's will. It is a process of surrender—releasing thoughts, desires, and emotions that pull us away from God's truth and embracing His perfect will.

Yielding to God is not a one-time decision but a continual journey—one that sharpens our ability to hear the Holy Spirit and deepens our trust in His leading. As Job declared: *"Though He slay me, yet will I trust Him"* (Job 13:15). Trusting God means daily choosing to let go of control, resting in His wisdom, and aligning ourselves with His purposes.

When we surrender every part of ourselves to Him, He equips us to walk with clarity and strength despite our human weaknesses.

In these moments of stillness and expectation, our anxious thoughts give way to His peace. As our hearts quiet before Him, we come into greater agreement with His voice and become more receptive to His leading.

As we walk in alignment with His Spirit, we begin to experience the mystery of oneness with Him.

Galatians 5:24-25 reminds us: *"And those who are Christ's have crucified the flesh with its passions and desires. If we live in the Spirit, let us also walk in the Spirit."*

Walking in the Spirit means learning to quiet the demands of our human nature and instead follow His voice. Paul expressed this ongoing process in 1 Corinthians 15:31, saying,

"I die daily." This daily yielding to Jesus's guidance allows His Spirit to fill us with peace that surpasses all understanding (Philippians 4:7). When we entrust every part of ourselves to Him, He strengthens us, giving us clarity and stability even in our weakness.

True peace is found in this alignment—when our soul serves the spirit rather than striving for control. As we consistently choose obedience over self-reliance, we cultivate a deep, personal relationship with the Holy Spirit. This intentional walk positions us to experience the fullness of God's peace, power, and purpose in our lives.

The Beauty of Weakness: Power in Surrender

Recognizing our weaknesses and limitations is not a sign of failure but an opportunity to be empowered by His divine strength. When we stop striving in our own strength and surrender to God, His peace begins to flow into our lives, replacing anxiety and striving with His love and rest. Our weakness is not a design flaw but a place for God's grace to work in us. It is in our weakness that we truly discover our dependence on Him, understanding that apart from Him, we can do nothing (John 15:5).

This surrender allows us to receive His grace, strength, peace, and the fruit of His Spirit—qualities that flow freely when we are rooted in His presence. Our weaknesses are not a sign of failure but an invitation for the Holy Spirit to work in and through us. Like Paul in 2 Corinthians 12, true strength comes from realizing our dependence on God, which allows His power to be made perfect in our weakness.

When we embrace this truth, we stop resisting and start resting in Him, which leads to a life marked by His peace and purpose. But resting in Him does not mean passivity; rather, it prepares our hearts for a deeper, expectant waiting—a posture of trust that actively seeks His presence and direction.

Waiting in His Presence

The Hebrew word for *"wait"* (qavah) speaks to an active, expectant waiting. It's not a passive sitting back but a deliberate, intentional act of surrender. This waiting is a posture of trust and hope, where we anticipate God's presence and guidance with confidence. As we wait in His presence, our spirits align with His, making us more sensitive to His guidance and direction.

Spirit intertwining is not just a theoretical concept; it is a tangible spiritual reality. Through intentional surrender, we allow the Holy Spirit to intertwine with our spirits, drawing us into deeper communion with God. This process of waiting refines us, quiets our inner turmoil, and ushers in God's peace, which strengthens and sustains us.

The Mystery of Oneness with Him

This mystery is revealed through our spiritual rebirth—being born again and made new in Christ. Our old selves are crucified, and we are raised to new life with Him, united in a relationship that transforms us from the inside out. The Holy Spirit now dwells within us, guiding us in truth, filling us with peace, and aligning us with God's heart.

As we move in step with the Holy Spirit, we begin to sense His timing and direction—not only in prayer but in every area of life. Walking in oneness with Him means seeking His wisdom in all things, allowing His presence to shape our decisions, actions, and words so they reflect His love and truth. This process draws us into a deeper intimacy with God, where His power, purpose, and peace flow through every part of our being.

This journey transforms our hearts and expands our capacity to bring His light and love into the world. As we surrender to the Holy Spirit, we stop striving in our own strength and learn to live fully surrendered to His will—the essence of a Spirit-led life.

Surrendering to the Spirit: A Continuous Journey

Taking up our cross daily (Luke 9:23) means choosing God's will over our personal preferences and plans. This act of self-denial is not burdensome when viewed through the lens of love and trust in God's perfect plan. It is essential for spiritual growth and developing greater sensitivity to the Holy Spirit's guidance.

When we yield to God, we allow the Holy Spirit to shape our hearts, minds, and decisions, glorifying God and benefiting us in the process. This surrender replaces our striving with the peace of knowing we are walking in His will, free from the pressure of trying to do things in our own strength.

Being led by the Holy Spirit is a continuous, transformative journey. As we exchange our will for God's, we create space for the Spirit to work within us, renewing our minds, shaping our character, and aligning our hearts with His purposes. This process allows us to experience the intertwining of spirits, making us more attuned to His voice and responsive in obedience. The essence of being led by the Spirit—the core principle—is to live in constant surrender and obedience to His guidance.

The story of Jesus in the Garden of Gethsemane, where He prayed: *"Not My will, but Yours be done"* (Luke 22:42), stands as the ultimate model of trust and submission. In this moment of unimaginable personal cost, Jesus demonstrated the depth of obedience required to fully embrace God's plan. Similarly, we are called to submit our will to God daily, even when it's hard, when it doesn't align with our desires, or when it's difficult to understand.

This journey of surrender is an ongoing adventure. We continually lay down our own will at the foot of the cross, allowing Him to mold us into a greater likeness of Christ.

To walk in this divine relationship, we must release our desires, plans, and expectations to embrace God's better plan. By yielding fully to Him, we create space for His Spirit to guide us. It is here, in this surrender, that we find true freedom and purpose—by laying down what could hinder our growth and choosing His way over our own.

Healing and Deliverance for Restoring Peace

Before we can fully walk in the Spirit and experience the fullness of God's peace, we must confront the emotional wounds and spiritual strongholds that hinder our surrender. These wounds—whether from past trauma, unforgiveness, or even demonic oppression—create unrest in the soul, forming barriers that resist the Holy Spirit's healing work and rob us of the peace we are meant to carry.

Healing our minds, memories, and triggers (inner healing) and breaking free from demonic influence and attacks (deliverance) are essential steps in restoring peace to our hearts. These processes go beyond addressing past pain; they restore the soul to its rightful place under the guidance of the Spirit. Only when we allow the Holy Spirit to heal us and break the chains of oppression can we experience the freedom to walk in complete surrender to His will.

We invite the Holy Spirit to heal our hearts and restore our peace through prayer, repentance, and a willingness to surrender. Jesus promised: *"Peace I leave with you; My peace I give to you"* (John 14:27). This promise becomes a reality as we allow Him to remove the burdens that weigh us down and replace them with His perfect peace.

The journey of inner healing is not just about emotional relief; it is about spiritual renewal. As we confront our fears and explore our brokenness and traumatic memories with courage and compassion, we invite the Holy Spirit to work in the deepest parts of our souls. It is here, in these vulnerable places, that the peace of Christ restores every fragmented part of our being. When we allow the Holy Spirit to heal our wounds, we experience the peace that surpasses understanding (Philippians 4:7). This peace empowers us to walk in deeper intimacy with God, free from the disruptions that once held us captive.

True surrender comes from a heart at peace. When our souls are free from the burdens of past wounds or spiritual strongholds, we become more open to the Holy Spirit's guidance and are better equipped to live fully. Living in a Spirit-led way allows us to rise above human understanding and to trust deeply in God's wisdom. Peace serves as the foundation of surrender, enabling us to depend fully on God's will and to rest in His presence.

The Battle Between Flesh and Spirit

Living in the Spirit involves not only aligning our souls with God's will but also confronting the spiritual forces that wage war against us. The battle between the flesh and the Spirit is both internal and external. Internally, our soul wrestles with desires, emotions, and thoughts that conflict with God's purposes. Externally, the enemy seeks to disrupt our peace through pressures, temptations, and lies that challenge our faith and obedience. His goal is to steal our peace by creating doubt, fear, and confusion through circumstances, people, and situations designed to distract us from God's truth.

Victory isn't just about overcoming external attacks—it also means conquering the inner conflict that tries to rob us of peace. This ongoing process is a vital part of our transformation, drawing us into deeper intimacy with God, where we find refuge and protection from our true enemies. Surrendering to the Holy Spirit is not only an internal act; it requires active resistance against the spiritual forces that attempt to lead us astray. By standing firm in God's peace, we push back against the enemy's schemes and continue moving forward in the Spirit.

Though this battle can feel overwhelming, it's crucial to recognize that surrendering control is an intentional choice—one that opens the door to God's peace, even in the middle of conflict. It is a continual commitment to resist the lies of the enemy and embrace the truth of God's Word (James 4:7). When we stand firm in the peace of Christ; we actively defy the forces that try to pull us away from His presence.

Spiritual Disciplines for Victory

Spiritual disciplines such as prayer, fasting, and deliverance are essential tools for maintaining a yielded heart. Through these practices, we confront the enemy's lies with the truth of God's Word, refocusing our hearts on His peace. These disciplines equip us with the clarity, strength, and peace we need to walk by the Spirit, no matter the internal or external pressures we face.

As we yield to the Holy Spirit, we experience true victory and freedom—not through our own power but through God's strength within us.

A New Way of Walking: Learning Step-by-Step

Learning to walk in the Spirit is much like learning to walk as a child—it's a step-by-step process in which we continually seek His guidance in every decision. Just as a child carefully takes each step to avoid falling, we, too, must be mindful of our steps in the Spirit, trusting that He will lead us with peace in each moment.

I remember an afternoon when we first got barn kittens. They were so curious and playful, following me around wherever I went. As I moved, I had to be extra careful and aware, making sure I didn't accidentally step on them. Every step I took required my attention, adjusting my movements to avoid accidentally hurting them. As this was happening, the Holy Spirit used these kittens to speak to me about walking in sync with Him. Just as I needed to move carefully around the kittens, I realized I must stay aware of the Spirit's guidance, paying attention to where He leads and adjusting my steps accordingly. Walking in the Spirit requires the same careful attention—ensuring we don't cause harm to others or lose our connection with God's direction. It also keeps us safe, helping us avoid stumbling or going down paths that could lead to harm.

This means regularly seeking God's guidance, checking our hearts, and ensuring we are aligned with His will. When we do this, His peace guards our steps, even in uncertainty. And if we stumble, His grace is more than enough. Like a loving parent, He lifts us up, heals our wounds, and restores our peace, urging us to press on.

Each decision to trust God is a small but significant step toward spiritual maturity. As our trust deepens, so does our ability to discern His will and walk in the Spirit. Though the steps may seem small at first, they lead to a deeper intimacy with God, where peace becomes a constant companion and guide.

Pressing Into God's Call

In Philippians 3:13-14, Paul urges us to forget what lies behind and reach for what lies ahead, pursuing the higher purpose God has set before us in Christ Jesus. This challenge isn't about merely progressing but about advancing with determination and faith toward the divine calling on our lives. It's an invitation to actively seek a deeper, more intimate relationship with God, regardless of past struggles or victories. Our spiritual walk isn't static but dynamic, driven by God's call to go further, higher, and deeper.

Every step is a chance to leave our comfort zones and enter a deeper revelation of who God is. As we continue down this path, we do so with purpose, eager to explore the depths of His love, the richness of His grace, and the power of His presence. God constantly beckons us to move beyond shallow faith, inviting us into the unknown, where His deepest treasures are found. It's here, in His heart, that peace is discovered, even in uncertainty.

Revelation 4:1-2 captures this invitation: *"Come up here, and I will show you things which must take place after this."* Just as John was invited to ascend into a higher spiritual realm, we, too, are called to lift our perspective above the distractions of the world as we are seated with Christ in heavenly places. From this vantage point, we experience a peace that transcends earthly limitations, shifting how we live and move. We're no longer bound by circumstances but free to live in direct communion with God, where His perspective becomes our own.

In 2 Corinthians, we are reminded that as we behold the glory of the Lord, we are transformed into His image, from glory to glory, by the Spirit. Philippians assures us that God will complete the good work He has begun in us. However, this transformation isn't passive—it is an active, deeply personal process of yielding to God's will. Each time we submit to the Holy Spirit, we are reshaped to reflect Christ more clearly. The more we submit to His authority, the more His glory fills our hearts. This isn't just about external change; it is about deep, internal transformation—reshaping our desires, refining our thoughts, and aligning our actions with His will.

The weight of His glory calls for a deeper surrender. As we are granted more of His presence, we must be refined to carry it. This is the refining fire of God's love—purifying, strengthening, and preparing us for the unique purpose He has designed for our lives. Each act of surrender positions us to take on greater responsibility in His kingdom, revealing His glory through our lives and impacting the world around us.

As we continue this journey, we must remember that transformation is not about striving but about allowing the completed work of Christ to take effect in us. When we yield to God's will, embrace His timing, and trust His perfect plan, we experience the fullness of His transformative power. The goal is not merely to reach a destination but to be continually conformed to the image of Christ, living and moving in Him (Acts 17:28). In this process, His peace will guide us with every step we take.

Living in the Spirit: Access to Divine Revelations

Through Jesus, we have direct access to the Holy of Holies—a sacred place for deep communion with God. Colossians 2:3 reveals: *"In Him are hidden all the treasures of wisdom and knowledge."*

As we passionately pursue Him, we step into a realm where the mysteries of the Kingdom are unveiled. This deep, intimate knowledge of God is not merely informational—it is transformational. It shifts our hearts and minds, grounding us in His presence and leading us to lasting peace. The closer we draw to Him, the more He chisels away the dross, revealing our true identity in Christ. As we ascend into a higher realm of understanding that surpasses human wisdom, the deep things of God are made known to our hearts—shaping, renewing, and equipping us to walk in alignment with His will. This alignment brings peace—not just a fleeting emotion but a deep, abiding reality.

Proverbs 25:2 reminds us: *"It is the glory of God to conceal a matter, but the glory of kings is to search out a matter."*

God delights in raising us as His sons and daughters, inviting us to seek out the hidden treasures He has prepared for us. This pursuit is not about striving for insight or proving our worth; it is about becoming who He designed us to be—His beloved children, created to reflect His character and love. He calls us to be overcomers—bold, courageous, and deeply attuned to His heart. As we follow His guidance, we reflect His glory, fulfill His purposes, and walk in faith, knowing we are chosen, redeemed, and empowered by His Spirit.

Hebrews 11:6 assures us that God rewards those who diligently seek Him. Part of that reward is divine revelation—insight into cultivating peace, love, and spiritual gifts. This revelation is not just for personal growth but also to equip us to walk in the fullness of the Spirit, reflecting God's glory, advancing His Kingdom on Earth, and living in the peace He freely offers.

Through Jesus' sacrifice on the cross, the veil was torn, granting us continual access to His presence. This invitation is not a one-time event; it is a call to a deeper, ongoing relationship with Him through the Holy Spirit. As we commit ourselves to prayer, worship, and the Word, we open ourselves to a greater revelation of who He is and who He created us to be.

Entering the Holy of Holies: Deeper Intimacy

To walk in the Spirit, we must first understand and embrace who we truly are in Christ. —as God's beloved, fully forgiven, empowered by the Holy Spirit, and deeply connected to Him—forms the foundation of our surrender and obedience. When we fully acknowledge who we are in Him, we let go of the need for control, realizing that we are no longer defined by past mistakes or bound by the fleshly impulses that once held us captive. As 2 Corinthians 5:17

declares: *"If anyone is in Christ, he is a new creation; old things have passed away; behold, all things have become new."*

Embracing this new identity transforms our thinking, decisions, and way of life. Every act of surrender and each moment spent in God's presence draws us closer to His heart, stripping away the layers that once blinded us and revealing more of His Spirit within us. Recognizing His inherent goodness and unfailing love dispels every fear that could extinguish the fire of our hearts for Him.

The *'Mountain of Amana'* in Song of Solomon 4:8 symbolizes the spiritual heights we are called to reach in our relationship with God. Just as the bride in Song of Solomon transitions from longing to fulfillment in the presence of her beloved, we, too, are invited to deepen our union with Christ. This journey is not about seeking His blessings but about desiring Him above all else.

True intimacy with God is not measured by what we receive from Him but by how earnestly our hearts long to be near Him—surpassing everything this world offers. As we bring our hearts into harmony with His, we become more attuned to the Holy Spirit's guiding voice, learning to trust His lead and follow His direction with unwavering faith.

Walking in the Spirit is a continual invitation to ascend higher—to know God more intimately and experience the fullness of His presence. This ascent is not merely an outward pursuit but a profound, life-changing journey that aligns our hearts with His—where true peace and lasting fulfillment are found.

Conclusion: Surrendering to the Spirit's Work

As you reflect on the truths shared in this chapter, take a moment to consider where you are on your journey of living and walking in the Spirit. Are there areas in your life where you've been holding back from fully surrendering to God's will? Are there struggles, fears, or insecurities that have caused you to resist His leading?

Walking in the Spirit is not just a one-time decision but a daily choice—a continual invitation to yield to the Holy Spirit's work in your life. It is about stepping into the abundant peace and purpose God has prepared for you. The peace that surpasses all understanding is not a distant dream but a present reality when you surrender to Him. In His presence, you find rest, strength, and guidance for every step of the journey.

This path of surrender is a powerful, ongoing transformation. It invites you to grow in intimacy with God, develop deep discernment, and bear the fruit of the Spirit. The Holy Spirit is actively at work within you, shaping you into the likeness of Christ and equipping you to walk in His peace, joy, and strength.

Each day you choose to walk in the Spirit, you will find that the gifts and fruit you seek are not just outcomes but the natural byproducts of an intimate relationship with Him.

Yield to His will and watch as your life overflows with peace that transforms the joy that strengthens and power that aligns you with God's divine purpose.

As you deepen your walk with Him, trust that He is guiding you toward a peace that heals what is broken and empowers you to live boldly. Your life will become a testimony to His faithfulness, reflecting the power of His presence in every step.

Let your life bear witness to the restoration that comes from walking in step with the Spirit. Know that as you surrender, you are moving deeper into the fullness of God's plan for your life. You are never alone on this journey—the Holy Spirit is with you, guiding, empowering, and transforming you into the likeness of Christ. *"This is the way, walk in it"* (Isaiah 30:21).

Invitation to Surrender

As you reflect on these steps, invite the Holy Spirit to search your heart and gently reveal any areas that need surrender. Offer those areas to Him with a willing and open spirit, asking for His wisdom, guidance, and strength to walk fully in His leading. This act of trust deepens your relationship with God and aligns your heart with His purpose.

Take a moment to breathe deeply and pray:

Holy Spirit, I open my heart to You today. Reveal anything in my life that I have not fully surrendered. I release my fears, doubts, and desires into Your hands, trusting Your goodness and wisdom. Guide me to walk closely with You, to recognize Your voice, and to follow wherever You lead. Fill me afresh with Your power and peace, that my life may bear the fruit of Your Spirit and reflect Your love. I surrender all that I am to You. Have Your way in me, Lord. In Jesus' name, Amen.

Seven
The Power of Perspective

Perspective shapes everything. How we view the world around us determines how we respond to it. A slight shift in our perspective can change how we interpret challenges and experience peace.

The Power of Perspective

The ultimate shift in perspective comes when we stop seeing life through our limited lens and begin to see it through God's eternal viewpoint—one that holds infinite clarity and wisdom. The Holy Spirit invites us to align with heaven's perspective, transforming how we face each day, trusting in God's sovereignty, and actively engaging in His Kingdom here on earth.

Understanding God's Perspective

God's perspective is the foundation for walking in peace because it transcends the limitations of what we can see in the natural world. His ways are not bound by time, space, or circumstances but are grounded in His eternal wisdom and unfailing love. Recognizing the difference between our viewpoint and God's allows us to embrace His sovereignty over all situations. In Isaiah 55:8–9 we are reminded of this divine difference: *"For My thoughts are not your thoughts, nor are your ways My ways,"* says the Lord. *"For as the heavens are higher than the earth, so are My ways higher than your ways, and My thoughts than your thoughts."*

God sees the beginning and the end—He holds the entire picture in His hands. While we may feel overwhelmed by the moment, He is working beyond what we can see, bringing everything into alignment with His divine plan.

Romans 8:28 reassures us: *"And we know that all things work together for good to those who love God, to those who are the called according to His purpose."* Even when circumstances feel unclear or painful, we can rest in the truth that God's perspective is perfect. This assurance frees us from the grip of fear and empowers us to lean into His peace, trusting that His plans are far greater than we can imagine.

Paul further encourages us in 2 Corinthians 4:17–18, saying: *"For our light affliction, which is but for a moment, is working for us a far more exceeding and eternal weight of glory, while we do not look at the things which are seen, but at the things which are not seen. For the things which are seen are temporary, but the things which are not seen are eternal."*

When we start to understand life from God's eternal perspective, we shift our focus from the temporary to the eternal. We begin to realize that our struggles are not random but rather a vital part of a greater, divine story unfolding in God's perfect plan.

God's will is always good and perfect, even when it seems mysterious or difficult to understand. Romans 12:2 calls us to: *"Be transformed by the renewing of your mind, that you may prove what is that good and acceptable and perfect will of God."*

When we let go of our need to understand every detail and choose to trust His vision, our perspective changes. As we align ourselves with His eternal viewpoint, we release our limited understanding in exchange for the gift of seeing through His eyes—a perspective that encompasses generations and eternity.

This transformation radically changes how we approach life's challenges, enabling us to embrace His peace regardless of the situation. His peace becomes our anchor, empowering us to walk confidently in His divine purpose. With God's perspective, we can face life with calm assurance, knowing that His eternal plan is unfolding even when the road ahead is unclear.

Recognizing God's Sovereignty

Gaining God's perspective involves realizing that He is sovereign over all things. Nothing happens outside His ultimate control or permission, and this truth provides immeasurable peace to those who embrace it. Psalm 103:19 affirms: *"The Lord has established His throne in heaven, and His kingdom rules over all."*

Trusting in God's sovereignty means recognizing that, no matter how overwhelming or even horrific our circumstances may seem, He remains in control and has a good plan for those called according to His purpose. When we grasp this truth, fear and anxiety lose their grip on our hearts. Challenges become opportunities to rest in His greater plan, and we find the strength to face difficulties with boldness, knowing they serve His divine purpose in our lives.

In moments when life feels chaotic or out of control, it's easy to lose sight of God's sovereignty. Sometimes, disobedience or following our own shortsighted plans opens the door to the enemy's attacks. Satan would love nothing more than for us to blame God for the consequences of stepping outside His will. Yet, even in these situations, God is neither surprised nor unprepared. He sees the end from the beginning, and through His grace and mercy, He has already made provisions for our redemption. Isaiah 46:10 reminds us of God's declaration: *"I declare the end from the beginning, and from ancient times reveal what is still to come. My purposes will stand, and I will accomplish all that I desire."*

He has the ability to bring His plans to fruition. When we repent—turning back to Him and surrendering everything into His hands—He redeems not only our circumstances but also us, including the time we've wasted. Trusting in His sovereignty means believing that nothing is wasted. Every struggle, every delay, and every heartbreak is skillfully woven into His greater tapestry. While we may not see the finished product until we reach heaven, we trust in the goodness of the Master weaver.

From God's perspective, every piece of His divine plan is already perfectly in place. When we align with His sovereignty, we exchange confusion for clarity and fear for peace. This trust allows us to walk in freedom, knowing that every step—even the missteps—is being used for His glory and our ultimate good.

Aligning with God's Will

Shifting to God's point of view requires intentionally seeking His guidance through prayer, meditating on Scripture, and listening to the Holy Spirit. Proverbs 3:5-6 encourages us: *"Trust in the Lord with all your heart, and lean not on your own understanding; in all your ways acknowledge Him, and He shall direct your paths."*

Aligning with God's will requires us to surrender our own agendas to fully embrace His. When we agree with His vantage point, we begin to think and respond as He does. Our hearts become more discerning of His voice, and His peace replaces any lingering fears. This alignment enhances our trust in Him and strengthens our ability to hear Him clearly, equipping us to confront any obstacles with wisdom and confidence.

When we walk in harmony with God, we are no longer overwhelmed by uncertainty. Instead, we navigate life with peace of mind, trusting that He guides our every step and orchestrates all things for our ultimate good.

The Role of Wisdom

Wisdom is a precious gift from God that enables us to navigate life with clarity and purpose. James 1:5 invites us to ask for wisdom, promising that God will provide it generously. Wisdom allows us to look beyond the surface, unveiling the deeper divine plan and revealing the meaningful reasons behind every situation.

For instance, divine wisdom often brings peace during decision-making. It may not always provide immediate answers, but it offers a sense of tranquility or a gentle nudge in the right direction. Even when the full outcome is unclear, this peace rests upon us, helping us handle dilemmas with emotional maturity and increased trust. As we seek and receive wisdom, our trust in God deepens, guiding us into His peace—peace that surpasses understanding and aligns us with His will and purposes.

I remember a prophetic word given to me, saying that I would face some big decisions that year. Immediately, fear gripped my heart. I hadn't made many wise decisions in my life, and I doubted how I would ever discern God's will in such uncertain circumstances. But during that fear, something unexpected happened—peace. It wasn't logic or the circumstances around me that brought clarity; it was God's peace resting deeply within me. I realized that peace wasn't merely the absence of anxiety; it was the presence of God guiding me. In that moment, I learned that God's peace—rather than my own understanding or sight—was the true compass for making decisions.

The Holy Spirit plays a vital role in imparting God's wisdom. As Jesus promised in John 16:13a: *"However, when He, the Spirit of truth, has come, He will guide you into all truth."*

Often, this guidance comes in stillness—when the Spirit brings a Scripture to mind or provides a quiet confirmation in our hearts. It may also come through another person, a sermon, a song, or even a subtle unction, all of which lead us into His peace.

Applying wisdom isn't about having every detail figured out—it's about placing unwavering trust in God with each step we take. As we surrender to His leading, godly wisdom transforms the way we approach relationships, work, and personal growth, anchoring us in His perspective and will. With every decision, we are grounded in His peace, knowing that His plan is unfolding perfectly, even when we can't see the full picture.

Living from a Higher Perspective

When we embrace God's perspective, we begin to live with confidence in His sovereignty, wisdom, and timing. This higher perspective allows us to rise above temporary struggles and focus on eternal realities. One of the key ways we can achieve this is by learning to wait on the Lord. Waiting is not passive inactivity but an active expression of trust in His perfect sovereignty and timing. Isaiah 40:31 reminds us: *"But those who wait on the Lord shall renew their strength; they shall mount up with wings like eagles, they shall run and not be weary, they shall walk and not faint."*

This verse teaches us that waiting on God does not make us stagnant; instead, it renews us, building resilience and endurance. Just as eagles soar above the storm, waiting in God's presence lifts us above the turbulence of life's temporary struggles, providing us with the spiritual strength to press on.

Waiting is essential to embracing God's higher perspective. In waiting, we are strengthened, refined, and taught to trust His wisdom over our own limited understanding. It is here that our vision shifts—where we stop focusing on the immediate and begin aligning our hearts with what is eternal, understanding that every moment of waiting is part of His perfect plan.

Waiting, then, becomes an opportunity to abide in God—to intentionally remain in His presence with hope and expectation. Psalm 91:1 declares: *"He who dwells in the secret place of the Most High shall abide under the shadow of the Almighty."*

Abiding in God's shadow is a place of safety and trust. It shifts our focus from unmet desires to the One who holds all things together. It allows us to rise above temporary struggles and face them with the spiritual stamina that only comes from being rooted in God's presence. Abiding transforms waiting from a time of frustration into a sacred time of preparation, where God renews our hearts, strengthens our faith, and aligns us with His purposes and insights.

Waiting in this way invites deeper intimacy with God, turning delays into divine moments of trust. During these times, we are grounded in His peace and confident in His perfect plan. Philippians 4:6–7 reminds us to present our anxieties to God in prayer, assuring us that His peace will guard our hearts and minds, teaching us to capture every negative thought, and providing us with the strength to stand firm on God's word and promises, regardless of the challenges that arise.

At times, the fruit of our obedience may not be immediately visible. Consider the prophetic words of Isaiah concerning the coming of Jesus, which were fulfilled 700 years later, or the promise God made to Abraham—that his descendants would be as numerous as the grains of sand—though Abraham never witnessed the full realization of that promise in his lifetime. Yet, both trusted in God's faithfulness beyond what they could see.

Likewise, we are called to trust in God's goodness and cling to His promises, confident that His plans are always good because He is good.

This higher perspective invites us to think beyond the present moment—to see our lives as part of a greater legacy, one that impacts not just today but generations to come. When we live with this perspective, peace replaces anxiety, and we find joy in knowing that even the smallest acts of obedience are woven into God's eternal, perfect plan.

Conclusion: The Power of Perspective

A shift in perspective changes everything. When we align with God's viewpoint, we gain the wisdom, peace, and trust needed to navigate life's challenges. With a heavenly perspective, we see beyond the surface, understanding that God's plans are always for our good, even when the path seems unclear. This alignment helps us live from a place of faith rather than fear, and wisdom becomes the lens through which we interpret life, grounding us in eternal truths instead of fleeting emotions or temporary struggles.

The process of realignment is ongoing, but with each step, we grow in clarity and strength, trusting God's perfect timing and sovereignty. As we embrace His perspective, we experience the profound peace that comes from knowing He is at work in every area of our lives—both in us and through us. Living with heaven's eyes allows us to rise above what is seen and focus on what is unseen and eternal, shifting our mindset from striving to resting, from fear to faith, and from short-term thinking to eternal purpose.

Ultimately, embracing God's perspective transforms the way we live. It positions us to have greater confidence in Him, navigate life's complexities with godly wisdom and patience, and walk confidently in His perfect plan. Life's challenges may not always make sense, but when we live from God's perspective, we remember that we are part of His grand, eternal story. This perspective empowers us to live with godly purpose, peace, and power, trusting that each small act of obedience contributes to His greater plan—a plan that is infinitely good and eternally perfect.

Eight
Restoring Peace

Have you ever felt like your life was in pieces—so broken that nothing seemed to make sense anymore? Restoration, in the biblical sense, is not just about mending what's torn. It's about making something beautiful from the fragments, something only God can envision.

Peace as Restoration: God's Work of Wholeness

As we explored earlier, Biblical peace—or shalom—is far more than the absence of strife. It encompasses healing, reconciliation, completeness, and the restoration of all things to their intended wholeness in God.

God's healing work is a divine act of restoration, mending what is lost or broken and making it whole. This restoration goes beyond returning to an original state—it involves an abundance of grace, bringing about a newness that surpasses the former. Scripture repeatedly speaks of this kind of transformation. As believers, we are invited to partner with God in bringing His Kingdom's order, healing, and wholeness to every area of life.

God's promise of restoration transcends our mistakes, regrets, and failures. His sovereignty is not bound by time or circumstance. Though He calls us to live fully in the present, He can reach into the past to heal wounds, redeem brokenness, and transform what seemed irreparable into something filled with purpose and beauty. When God restores, He does so beyond the limits of human understanding or imagination. He is our Redeemer, capable of turning ashes into beauty, mourning into joy, and despair into hope (Isaiah 61:3).

Consider a broken vase. If we attempt to glue it back together without the input of a master artist, it will remain flawed and never quite the same. But in God's hands, the vase is not only restored; it is made whole. The cracks become channels for His light to shine through, creating a masterpiece more beautiful than the original. He doesn't merely mend; He elevates, perfects, and reveals His glory in ways we could never envision.

Like the Japanese art of Kintsugi, where a master artist uses gold to fill in cracks, making the repaired pottery even more valuable through its strength and beauty, God does the same—and even better—with the cracks in our hearts and lives.

Biblical Foundations of Restoration

Many Biblical stories, including Job and Joel's, beautifully illustrate the truth of God's restorative power. Each story reveals God's ability to redeem, renew, and restore on both personal and collective levels.

Job: Restoration After Suffering

Job's story is a profound testament to restoration following an unimaginable loss. A man of integrity and deep faith, Job endured a cascade of devastating events—losing his wealth, health, and family. In his pain, Job wrestled with God, questioned his circumstances, and struggled to find meaning in his suffering. Yet, even amidst his deepest despair, Job never let go of his faith.

In the end, God's restoration surpassed human comprehension. Not only did He restore Job's fortunes—doubling what he had lost—but He also blessed him with a renewed family and a long, full life. Yet the greatest restoration was spiritual. Job declared, *"I have heard of You by the hearing of the ear; but now my eye sees You"* (Job 42:5). Job's journey teaches us that restoration comes through perseverance, trust, and surrender, even when we cannot see the purpose in our pain.

God's work in Job's life reminds us that no matter how broken our situation may seem, His power to restore is greater than the depth of our loss. When we hold fast to Him, even in the darkest valleys, He can turn our suffering into a testimony of His faithfulness and abundance.

Through suffering, we are refined and elevated, turning our theoretical understanding into a profound, personal awareness of His goodness.

Joel: God's Promise of Redeeming the Lost Years

While Job's story reveals restoration on a personal level, the prophet Joel speaks to God's ability to restore entire nations and redeem lost time. In Joel 2:25, God promises Israel: *"I will restore to you the years that the swarming locust has eaten"*. This declaration came after a catastrophic locust plague that left the land desolate, crops destroyed, and the people's future uncertain.

Joel called the nation to repentance, urging them to turn to God with fasting, prayer, and humility. In response, God's mercy overflowed with a promise of restoration: barren lands would flourish, harvests would overflow, and the people's spirits would be renewed. Joel's words remind us of God's extraordinary power—not just to replace what was lost, but to redeem time itself. He restores wasted seasons into fruitful harvests and changes despair into abundance.

You might be asking, "I know God can do this, but will He? And will He do it for me?" It's a natural question, one that I have personally wrestled with, especially when we can't see how our circumstances could ever change. But let me assure you: His promises are not just for others—they are for YOU, too. Even if you can't see it right now, even if your heart feels heavy with doubt or disappointment, especially if you feel hopeless, God is at work in ways beyond what we can understand. The restoration He offers is not limited by what has happened in the past; it is part of His perfect plan for your life right now.

If you're struggling to see how this could apply to you, I encourage you to ask God for a personal promise to carry you through. He delights in meeting you where you are and giving you a word of hope that speaks directly to your heart. Lean into His presence and trust that He will provide the assurance you need to keep walking in faith.

God's promises are not confined to biblical times; they are alive and active today. He is the same yesterday, today, and forever. Just as God restored in Scripture, God can and does restore broken years, lost opportunities, and shattered dreams now. His ability to bring healing and renewal knows no limits, and His timing is perfect. When you turn to Him—no matter where you are or how long it's been—He will meet you with grace and begin to redeem what seemed lost. You may not see it yet, but trust that His restoration is already at work, making all things beautiful in His time.

Personal Journey of Restoration

Have you ever looked at your situation and thought it was hopeless? I have. I tried everything to fix what was broken, but nothing seemed to work—or so I believed. I searched for signs, even the smallest hint that God was working. Ultimately, restoration boiled down to faith and trust. Did I believe in His promise? Yes. Did I see it? No. Did I feel it? Absolutely not. Yet, like Job, I clung to God's Word, declaring His promises over my situation.

There were times when I felt the weight of failure and loss, whether in relationships, dreams, or circumstances. But God's restoration isn't just about reclaiming the past; it's about stepping into the hope-filled future He has already planned for you. Restoration is not earned through good behavior or effort—but rather, it is a gift from our loving Father, who, in His grace, is able to redeem even the consequences of our mistakes and disobedience. While our actions have consequences, God's restorative power is greater than our failures. His love and mercy work in and through our brokenness, bringing healing and renewal.

I remember feeling like my life was a puzzle scattered across the floor. Pieces were missing, and I didn't know where to start. Yet, in those moments of despair, God was at work, gathering the pieces to build something eternal. His plans were greater than my own, and He was leading me into a new chapter—one I couldn't have imagined.

Restoration in the Waiting

Waiting for restoration can feel like planting a seed in the soil, buried beneath the earth, unseen to the naked eye. You can't see the growth happening, but beneath the surface, deep roots are forming, and the plant is being prepared to rise. The seed doesn't struggle in the soil—it simply trusts the process, knowing that in time, it will break through the ground and bloom.

Similarly, waiting for God's restoration can feel like a season of hidden growth. Even when it seems like nothing is happening on the surface, God is actively working in your heart and life, preparing you for the fullness of His promise. Waiting isn't about passively enduring—it's a time of development, where God is shaping and refining you to flourish in the future He has planned.

In the waiting, we learn to abide in Him, staying connected to the vine, even when the seasons feel dry and barren (John 15:4). God doesn't waste the waiting. His timing is always perfect, and He is never late. In God's perfect timing, restoration will spring forth—more beautiful and abundant than you could have imagined.

Shalom Reflection: Beauty from Ashes

God's peace restores what's broken, turning disorder into harmony. Restoration transforms brokenness into wholeness, creating beauty from ashes. As Isaiah 61:3 promises,

He gives: *"the oil of joy for mourning, the garment of praise for the spirit of heaviness."*

Take a moment to reflect: Where do you need God's restoration in your life? How can you partner with Him to restore your relationships and surroundings today? Trust in His power to redeem and restore, knowing that no situation is too far gone. In His hands, even the most shattered fragments can be remade into masterpieces. Let His restoring love flow through you, revealing His glory and drawing others into His Kingdom.

Conclusion

God's work of restoration is far more than a return to what was—it is a journey of transformation, healing, and new beginnings. Through His peace, He not only mends what is broken but elevates it to something more beautiful than we could ever imagine. His restoration is not bound by time, circumstances, or human understanding. It is rooted in His infinite love, and it brings hope to even the most hopeless situations.

As we reflect on His promises in Scripture—through the lives of Job, Joel, and countless others—we are reminded that restoration often follows perseverance and trust. Even in the darkest moments, God is at work. He is not only redeeming our past but also shaping our future. We are invited to partner with Him in this divine work, bringing

His Kingdom's peace into the broken places of our lives and the world around us.

The journey of restoration is not always easy, but it is always worth it. As you move forward, remember that God's love is powerful enough to redeem every broken part of your life, pour the healing balm of Gilead into all the cracks and crevices, restore beauty from the ashes, and bring about a peace that surpasses all understanding. Trust in His perfect timing, remain anchored in His Word and embrace the renewal He offers.

Restoration is not a singular event but an ongoing journey. It requires us to actively engage with God, continually surrendering our brokenness and partnering with Him in His transformative work. Below are powerful steps to deepen your journey of restoration—moving beyond routine practices to a place of true, lasting healing and peace.

Surrender Your Brokenness in Prayer

Restoration starts with surrendering the parts of your life that feel most broken and beyond repair. These are the areas where you've held onto control, and they often include wounds you've tried to hide or avoid. Invite God into these spaces, asking Him to restore not just the surface but the very core of your being.

Action: Set aside time to pray through your deepest hurts and fears. Ask God to reveal the areas where you've struggled to trust Him and invite His restoration into those places. Ask God to reveal where He was in those memories, too, allowing Him to show you His presence in the pain. This can bring deeper healing and clarity as you walk through the process of restoration.

Example Prayer:

Lord, I submit my brokenness to You. I have borne wounds I cannot heal by myself. Heal me from the inside out and restore what has been lost. I trust You with every part of my being.

Allow God to Heal Root Causes

Restoration involves more than just repairing visible damage—it encompasses addressing the underlying causes of pain, unforgiveness, and brokenness. At times, we hide these feelings deep within, but God's restoration process encourages us to look beyond the surface. He desires to reach the deepest parts of our hearts, providing healing where we need it most.

Now, I encourage you to reflect on these questions: What areas of your life require God's restoration today? Where can you find His peace for your brokenness? No matter how shattered things may appear, God offers His restoration to all who seek Him. Let us move forward in faith, trusting that in the Master's hands, every broken piece can transform into a masterpiece.

Nine
Anchored in Rest

In the stillness of rest, we find the strength to
move forward. Rest is not inactivity; it is the
divine pause where God's peace empowers us
to live fully without striving.

Rest is one of the most powerful yet often overlooked tools
God has given us for walking in peace. In a world that
demands hustle, striving, and performance, embracing rest
can feel counterintuitive. However, rest is neither laziness

nor passivity. It is a spiritual posture that opens the door to God's peace, even amid life's challenges.

The Lord once showed me a picture of a hammock to illustrate this truth. A hammock stays secure due to the tension on either side. If one side isn't anchored, the hammock collapses. This vision beautifully illustrates how tension, when anchored properly, creates a space for us to rest. The trees to which the hammock is tied provide the security and strength needed to support it. These trees represent God's promises, His unwavering faithfulness, His Word, and His power.

In our lives, we have anchors of faith and trust in God. These anchors support us through the tensions we face from family, work, relationships, or personal growth. Instead of allowing these tensions to overwhelm us, we can use them to create space for renewal by surrendering them to God and intentionally inviting Him into our situations. Rest is not about eliminating the tension but about trusting that God's peace will sustain us through it.

The hammock, supported by the strength of the trees, serves as a reminder that rest isn't about escaping life's challenges but about trusting in God's promises to hold us steady through them. Divine rest is an active alignment with God's perfect harmony and abundant life. It is a choice to lean into the strength of His promises, just as we would lean back into the support of a hammock. When we do, we experience a peace that surpasses understanding and find calm assurance, regardless of what life brings.

Rest as a Tool for Walking in Peace

Jesus beautifully modeled rest for us. In Mark 4:35-41, we find Him sleeping in a boat during a violent storm. As the waves crashed and fear gripped the disciples, they woke Him, exclaiming: *"Teacher, do You not care that we are perishing?"* In response, Jesus rose, rebuked the wind, and commanded the sea, *"Peace, be still!"* Immediately, the storm obeyed, and a great calm followed.

What stands out most about this moment is that Jesus remained at rest both before and during the storm. His peace did not depend on the absence of chaos but was anchored in His unwavering trust in the Father. He invites us to live with this same peace, rooted not in our circumstances but in God's unchanging character.

We often think we'll find rest "when"—when the problem is solved, when the workload eases, or when life feels manageable. But Jesus didn't wait for external peace before resting; He carried peace within Him. His rest was not passive or circumstantial—it was a declaration of trust, a refusal to be ruled by the storm.

This kind of rest isn't simply relief from exhaustion; it is a weapon against fear, a shield against anxiety, and a mark of deep faith. It is an act of war against the lie that says we must carry it all ourselves.

Genuine rest is not found in the absence of struggle but in the presence of the Father. He is El Shaddai—the All-Sufficient One—more than enough in every storm. When the winds rage and the waves rise, His rest is not shaken. It holds firm, unyielding, unbreakable. It is not a retreat from life's battles but the very place from which we fight and overcome.

Entering God's Rest

Hebrews 4:9-10 declares: "*There remains therefore a rest for the people of God. For he who has entered His rest has himself also ceased from his works as God did from His.*" This passage speaks not only of physical rest but also of spiritual rest—a ceasing from striving and instead surrendering to God's provision and grace.

When we stop trying to fix everything ourselves and instead lean into God's presence, we experience His supernatural peace. This doesn't mean we stop working or fulfilling our responsibilities altogether; it means we no longer bear them alone. We partner with God in obedience to His direction and allow Him to carry the weight. By trusting Him with the outcomes, we free ourselves to walk in His peace.

Rest Beyond Physical Relaxation

Scripture reveals that rest goes beyond physical relaxation, a break from work, or catching up on sleep. It is a deep, abiding peace that anchors us beyond our circumstances.

In Matthew 11:28-30, Jesus extends a life-changing invitation: *"Come unto me, all ye who labor and are heavy laden, and I will give you rest."* This invitation extends beyond physical exhaustion; it offers soul-refreshing peace that comes from surrendering our striving, anxieties, and fears to Him. It calls us to exchange the burdens we carry for the lightness of His grace.

True rest is a spiritual state that flows from trusting in God's sovereignty—a peace unshaken by external circumstances, providing stability and security no matter what we encounter. This soul-level rest is only attainable when we trust in the work that Christ has already completed on our behalf.

Embracing this rest means believing that God has already accomplished what is necessary for our well-being. Just as Jesus withdrew to pray and reconnect with His Father (Luke 5:16), we are called to rest in God's presence, drawing strength from Him instead of relying on our own efforts.

When we pause to seek Him, we realize that genuine peace isn't found in doing less but in surrendering more. Yielding to His love, abiding in His presence, and allowing His peace to settle deep within us brings a rest that cannot be shaken—one that remains steady no matter what storms arise.

Strengthened Through Rest

Ephesians 3:16 reminds us that God empowers us through His Spirit in our inner being: *"that He would grant you, according to the riches of His glory, to be strengthened with might through His Spirit in the inner man."* This inner strength flourishes in the quietness of His presence.

Rest is a divine exchange—our weakness for His unlimited strength, our striving for His unlimited peace. In these moments of surrender, our spirits are strengthened, equipping us to face life's challenges with confidence and courage from within.

The Spiritual Discipline of Rest

Finding rest in our fast-paced world requires intention and discipline. Our culture often glorifies striving and achievement, leaving little room for peace. However, the Bible teaches that true peace isn't something we fight for; it's something we enter into by faith.

Psalm 46:10 declares: *"Be still, and know that I am God."* This stillness goes beyond the absence of activity; it is a deliberate calming of our souls so that we can recognize and trust in God's sovereignty.

Hebrews 4:11 urges us: *"Let us therefore be diligent to enter that rest, lest anyone fall according to the same example of disobedience."* Choosing to disobey this invitation to rest is to resist God's design, which equips us to live in peace.

Jesus modeled this restful posture in His life, frequently retreating to quiet places to commune with His Father. We can follow His example through prayer, worship, and meditation on His Word—welcoming God's peace into our daily lives, not by escaping life's demands, but by inviting His presence into the midst of them.

Rest Trust in God's Sovereignty

Rest is an expression of trust. When we take time to rest, we declare that God is in control and choose to depend on His promises. Philippians 4:6-7 encourages us to trust in Him:

"Be anxious for nothing, but in everything by prayer and supplication, with thanksgiving, let your requests be made known to God; and the peace of God, which surpasses all understanding, will guard your hearts and minds through Christ Jesus."

When we entrust our worries to Him, His peace—strong and unwavering—serves as our shield. It not only comforts us but also steadies our souls with the deep assurance that God is good, His plans are trustworthy, and His provision is certain.

More than a pause from work, choosing rest is a declaration of faith—a willingness to surrender our lives to God's sovereignty. It is an ongoing practice of trusting Him and allowing His peace to rule over every area of our lives.

Our ability to rest depends on what we are anchored to. Just as a structure stands firm when secured to a solid foundation, our peace must be rooted in God's promises. His Word,

His presence, and His faithfulness sustain us through life's stresses. True rest isn't about escaping tension but trusting that God's truth will hold us steady.

Living from Rest: Practical Steps

Rest is more than a momentary escape; it is a way of life. To live in a place of peace, we must consistently trust God, meditate on His Word, and seek His presence throughout each day. This requires stepping away from the chaos and allowing His peace to wash over us. Whether through quiet prayer, worship, or simply sitting in stillness before Him, the key is to slow down and be fully present with God. True rest flows from intimacy with Him.

Rather than striving to control everything, embracing rest means recognizing the tensions in our lives and choosing to lean into God's presence. Just as a structure remains secure when firmly supported, we find stability in God's promises, His Word, prayer, and the Holy Spirit. These divine supports sustain us, providing the strength and peace we need to navigate life's challenges.

Conclusion: Rest as the Foundation for Revival

Rest is not a retreat; it's a weapon. It's a declaration of faith in a restless world and a radical alignment with God's Kingdom. By choosing to rest, we proclaim that God's strength is sufficient, His promises are unshakeable, and His presence is our greatest treasure. Rest is not merely a place where we find peace; it's where we are empowered to face life's battles with His Spirit energizing us.

Imagine a life anchored in God's rest. When storms rage, we remain unshaken, showing a peace that defies logic—one that draws others to Christ. Rest is where we are refilled, restored, and prepared for the calling He has placed on our lives. It's where we hear His voice, receive His strategies, and become equipped to do His will with confidence and joy.

Kingdom warriors do not depend on their own strength; they operate in the power of divine rest. Living from that place means standing firm, deeply rooted in God's faith-fulness, and unshaken by life's pressures. His Word, His presence, and His grace sustain and empower us, enabling us to bring His peace into a chaotic world.

This is the call: to live from His rest, igniting the world around us with the fire of His peace. Rest is not just for you—it's His invitation to partner with Him in bringing heaven to earth. So, surrender the striving, silence the doubts, and lean back fully into His promises. The world is waiting for the peace that only comes from Him. Live it. Carry it. Spread it. And watch as His rest becomes a revival through you.

Ten

Worship: A Gateway to His Presence

Worship is not just a song but an invitation to encounter God's presence, where true peace is found.

Worship: An Invitation to God's Presence

The presence of God is everything. Worship isn't just a moment—it's our entrance into that sacred place where heaven touches earth. It extends beyond songs and rituals; worship is a divine invitation to commune with the living

God. In these moments, heaven intersects with earth, and our hearts are drawn into His perfect peace. It is here, in the atmosphere of His glory, that His power meets our deepest needs, bringing transformation, healing, and rest.

True worship aligns us with His will and shifts the atmosphere around us. It is a holy act of surrender, tuning our hearts to His holiness. As we exalt Him, we enter the presence of the One who holds all peace and victory. This divine encounter renews our minds, sharpens our spiritual hearing, and anchors our identity in Him.

Worship serves as a gateway to holiness. Through this sacred act, we invite the Father to purify our hearts and empower us to walk in obedience. Whether through quiet surrender or bold declarations of praise, each act of worship draws us closer to becoming like Jesus—set apart, discerning His voice, and filled with His power.

Worship as a Divine Calling

Worship is not merely a church tradition or religious act—it is a divine calling that transcends time, culture, and personal circumstances. From the very beginning, God has called His people to worship—not as a duty, but as a doorway into deep, abiding relationship with Him.

In Exodus 8:1 (NIV), God instructed Moses to go to Pharaoh and demand: *"Let my people go, so that they may worship me."* This was more than a cry for physical deliverance—it was a call to spiritual freedom. God was beckoning His people out of bondage—not just from slavery in Egypt, but from the grip of sin, oppression, and every distraction that hinders wholehearted devotion.

True worship leads to freedom. Whether it's fear, shame, hidden wounds, or the chaos of life pulling us in different directions, worship invites us to lay it all down. In surrender, we find true freedom.

In His presence, we encounter the One who breaks every chain. Worship becomes the key that unlocks the fullness of His peace, healing, and restoration. It shifts us from survival to communion, from captivity to intimacy, and from striving to rest.

The Transformative Power of Worship

When we worship, we acknowledge God's sovereignty over every aspect of our lives. Worship shifts our focus from the limitations of our circumstances to the limitless power of our Creator. It is a conscious decision to honor God with our words, thoughts, actions, and attitudes. True worship becomes an offering, a declaration that proclaims, "God, You are above all things. I surrender my will to Yours."

In worship, we align ourselves with God's purposes. As we lift our hearts in surrender, we are reminded of His unfailing faithfulness, limitless power, and overwhelming love. Worship becomes both the invitation and the vehicle to step deeper into the divine calling God has for us.

In His presence, every chain that binds our hearts and souls is broken. The anointing received in worship breaks chains of bondage. Fear is silenced, strongholds crumble, and freedom is released.

Just as the Israelites left Egypt and broke free from the chains of slavery, we are invited to release anything that holds us back and step into God's liberating presence through worship.

True Worship: In Spirit and Truth

Worship is more than an outward act—it is the very essence of who we were created to be: hearts fully aligned with God in spirit and in truth. As Jesus said in (John 4:23-24), *"But the hour is coming, and now is, when the true worshipers will worship the Father in spirit and truth; for the Father is seeking such to worship Him. God is Spirit, and those who worship Him must worship in spirit and truth."*

As we see in Acts 2, the disciples were gathered in one accord—literally single-minded—awaiting the promise of the Holy Spirit. Worship unites us in one mind and one passion, bringing us into harmony with the presence of God. When we welcome the Spirit of God through wholehearted praise, Heaven invades Earth. The glory of God descends, releasing His profound peace, healing, and miracles.

This can happen both corporately and individually in your prayer room. God promises that wherever two or three are gathered, He is present among them (Matthew 18:20). When we gather in worship, whether in a shared space or alone before Him, worship connects us with God—through prayer, praise, and His abiding presence.

When we linger in worship, we develop a deeper passion for the things of God. Seeking Him in praise declares the battle cry of His truth—not only to our hearts but also to our circumstances and the world around us. Worship positions our hearts to receive Heaven's peace, yielding to His will and inviting Him to move in us and among us.

Worship is a Posture of the Heart

Worship is not about performance; it's about the posture of our hearts. Jesus said the Father seeks those who will worship in spirit and truth—not through outward actions alone, but through full surrender to His will. Worship aligns our hearts with His truth, making us more sensitive to His leading and more deeply rooted in His peace.

When we bow before God, we acknowledge His sovereignty. Worship begins in the heart but extends beyond words—it becomes action. It engages our entire being: hearts, minds, and bodies. As Psalm 95:6 states, *"Oh come, let us worship and bow down; let us kneel before the Lord our Maker."* In that moment of humility, we are uplifted by His power.

Worship aligns our spirits with the heart of God. True worship isn't about perfection; it's about connection. It is an invitation to draw near to the One who makes us whole, In that holy communion, we are renewed, strengthened, and equipped for His purpose. Worship creates space for His peace to reign—not only within us but over the storms that surround us.

Worship is more than a response; it is a declaration of war against the real enemy—Satan and his forces. It is a bold testimony of God's goodness and an act of faith in His power and breakthrough. In these times, worship becomes a powerful statement: Despite my circumstances, I choose to honor God.

2 Chronicles 20:22 shows us how worship dismantles strongholds and shifts the spiritual atmosphere. Worship isn't passive; it declares God's rule and releases His mighty power to move.

In worship, the fresh oil of the Spirit fills us—healing what is broken, restoring what is lost, and equipping us for the battles ahead. Worship ignites a fire within us—a fire that cannot be quenched. It is the fuel that keeps us going, even when the world tries to wear us down.

Worship is a Lifestyle of Gratitude

Worship isn't limited to a specific time, place, or physical posture—it's a way of life. It flows through every moment, shaping our thoughts, actions, and attitudes. True worship isn't just an activity; it's the rhythm of our very breath—a continual expression of gratitude that deepens our communion with Him.

In 1 Thessalonians 5:16–18, we are called to: *"Rejoice always, pray without ceasing, in everything give thanks; for this is the will of God in Christ Jesus for you."*

Just as the Israelites were called to worship in the wilderness through their struggles, challenges, and uncertainties, we, too, are invited to worship in every season. Worship is not just for times of joy and triumph; it carries us through barren, chaotic, and painful moments when God feels distant. In these times, worship becomes a bold declaration: despite my circumstances, I choose to honor God.

Each moment is an invitation—an opportunity to draw closer to God, experience His peace, and walk in His victory. A life of worship is a life of trust, where gratitude is our song and communion with Him is our home.

A Personal Encounter with Worship

I experienced the power of worship during one of my hardest seasons. I had been wrestling with loss and unanswered prayers, feeling distant from God—as if my faith had grown weary under the weight of my circumstances.

One Sunday morning, as I sat in church, I found myself unable to sing. I felt empty, as if I had nothing left to offer. Yet, in the silence, I heard His whisper: "I just want you. Not your performance, not your words. I want your heart."

At that moment, I realized that worship wasn't just about singing the right words or putting on a brave face—it was about surrendering. It wasn't about how strong I felt; it was about giving God my heart exactly as it was.

I started singing softly: "I surrender all."

It wasn't a loud declaration; it was raw, genuine, and vulnerable. Yet, in that moment of surrender, something shifted. God's peace began to fill me. The weight on my heart lifted, and I experienced His presence in a way I had never anticipated.

My circumstances didn't change instantly, but something within me did. Worship became my place of restoration—where my heart realigned with His holiness and my spirit was strengthened by His love.

Worship is not about the external; it is an internal surrender that transforms everything. It prepares our hearts to walk in holiness. As we worship in spirit and truth, we submit to His sovereignty, allowing Him to purify us and draw us closer to His voice. Worship is where our hearts align with His will.

The Power of Worship in the Battle for Peace

Worship is the key to breakthrough. It dismantles strongholds and shifts atmospheres. In 2 Chronicles 20, when the Israelites faced overwhelming odds, they turned to worship. The King of Israel told the people: *"Believe in the Lord our God, and you will be established."* He instructed them to *"position yourselves, stand still, and see the salvation of the*

Lord." This means they were to stand firm in their belief, hold their position, and watch God move on their behalf.

These ancient words echo across time as instructions for us today. We, too, are called to stand on God's promises, remain rooted in His peace, and receive His salvation and deliverance

Then something radical happened: The King then positioned the worshippers at the front of the battle, sending the praise team ahead of the armed forces: *"He appointed those who would sing to the Lord and praise the beauty of holiness as they went out before the army..."*

Worship went before warfare. Praise was the weapon instead of the sword.

This bold move demonstrated deep trust in God's instructions. Furthermore, it serves as a reminder that worship before the battle is an act of faith. It opens the door to sacred communion with our King, ushering us into the atmosphere of heaven, where His peace dispels fear and His glory reshapes our perspective.

In His presence, we stop measuring the size of our problems and start beholding the greatness of our God. Worship aligns our vision with His, enabling us to see the victory He's already secured.

Psalm 100:4 says: *"Enter His gates with thanksgiving, and His courts with praise."* Gates often symbolize decision points, while courts represent authority and legal matters.

Approaching both with thanksgiving and praise spiritually demonstrates our dependence on God and affirms our faith that He has already prepared the way for us to succeed.

In 2 Chronicles 20:22, we see how worship served as a catalyst for divine victory. As the people of Judah began to sing and praise, God moved mightily on their behalf, causing their enemies to turn against one another. Not a single enemy escaped. Worship unleashed the power of God's intervention, securing the victory without raising a sword.

Worship is the source of peace and victory, where God's strength empowers us to confront life's challenges. True worship represents a lifestyle that invites God's presence into every area of our lives. It transforms, strengthens, and enables us to embrace the victory He has already secured.

Worship is not passive; it is a weapon. It breaks chains, moves mountains, and declares God's triumph over every circumstance. When we worship, we align ourselves with His will, allowing His power to flow through us. Worship declares our dependence on God, enabling Him to make a way where none seems visible and to move on our behalf. When situations feel overwhelming, and we seem boxed in on every side, we just need to worship, trust in His promises, and praise Him in advance, believing His glory will come and shatter the enemy's best-laid plans.

Living with a Heart of Worship

Worship is the heartbeat of our spiritual walk, pulsing with the rhythm of grace and surrender. It is the continual posture of our hearts, the moment-by-moment decision to bow before God's greatness and acknowledge His sovereignty. Worship is not about striving for perfection but about being shaped and refined in the light of who He is. It is about authenticity.

When we come to God authentically, we bring our vulnerabilities and insecurities into the loving arms of the One who created us and knows us so intimately that He counts the hairs on our heads. We can trust that He desires what's best for us. The presence of such love naturally elicits a response of authentic worship.

When we worship in spirit and truth, we encounter God in the deepest parts of our being. Worship serves as a bridge between the heavenly and earthly realms, ushering us into deeper communion with the heart of God. When we meet the One who breathes life into us, everything changes. In Scripture, there is a clear shift in people's countenance, character, and circumstances after they have been with God. That same power is available to us today.

Let worship become your daily rhythm, as natural as breathing God's name. Let it be the fuel that sustains your spirit, the anchor that keeps you grounded, and the weapon that fights for your breakthrough. Worship is not just an act—it is the very gateway to the life of peace and victory that God has promised. As you worship, you align yourself with His purpose, His power, and His presence, walking in the fullness of all He has for you.

Conclusion

Worship is more than a song, more than lips filled with praise; it is the heartbeat of a life aligned with God. Through worship, we dwell in His presence, experience His peace, and access His power. It is the gateway to breakthrough—where strongholds are dismantled, hearts are renewed, and lives are forever changed.

As we embrace a lifestyle of worship, we deepen our connection with God—entering a realm of surrender, renewal, and divine intimacy. Worship is not confined to a church service; it is a daily invitation to create sacred space in every moment as we allow His will to shape our hearts. In His presence, we find a peace that surpasses all understanding—one that steadies us through life's storms.

Let worship be your weapon in times of struggle, your refuge in moments of chaos, and your joy in seasons of celebration. It is the key to unlocking the fullness of God's promises and encountering His perfect peace. As you cultivate a life of worship, you won't just stand in victory—you will carry His nearness into every circumstance.

Worship is the pathway to peace, the strength for your battles, and the unwavering assurance that God is with you—always.

Closing Commission

Walking in God's Peace

Now may the God of peace, who through the blood of the eternal covenant brought back from the dead our Lord Jesus, that great Shepherd of the sheep, equip you with everything good for doing His will, and may He work in us what is pleasing to Him, through Jesus Christ, to whom be glory forever and ever. Amen —Hebrews 13:20-21.

You are called to walk in a peace that shatters fear, silences storms, and declares the victory of Christ. This peace is not passive; it is a force that empowers you to stand firm, advance with courage, and transform every place you enter. Peace is not merely something to be received—it is a gift to be released.

You are a beloved child of God, entrusted with the authority of heaven. Clothed in His righteousness and empowered by His Spirit, you carry the atmosphere of heaven within you. His peace is not merely a shield; it is a sword that pierces the darkness and establishes His kingdom wherever you go.

I know things might feel overwhelming at times, but always remember that God sees you. He knows your struggles, and He is faithful to be with you in every circumstance. In your hardest moments, His peace will be your refuge, a constant source of comfort and strength. Keep trusting in Him, knowing that He is walking with you through every season and that His peace is greater than any storm you're facing.

As you move forward, I commission you to let your true identity be rooted in Him, to let your words be infused with grace, and your actions bear witness to His love, attracting others to the Prince of Peace. In difficult times, let your peace stand as a testament to those around you. During chaotic moments, may your peace provide calm and clarity, anchored in the very character of God.

I commission you to rest in His authority, fully surrendering your heart and mind to Him. As you embrace His perspective and trust in His perfect timing while walking in step with the Holy Spirit, may your vision align with heaven's view. Let His peace guard your heart and mind, flowing into every situation.

I commission you to walk in His holiness, to align your thoughts, feelings, and actions with God's truth, and to live by His Spirit as you surrender your flesh.

I commission you to walk with purpose, knowing that you are a vessel of divine peace. Every moment holds the potential to reflect His will. Let your life shine with His light.

I commission you to awaken to your calling and train your soul to walk in peace as you become one with His Spirit. May divine revelation and deep intimacy with the Living God be your portion.

I commission you to live from God's eternal perspective and walk in supernatural wisdom.

I commission you to receive full restoration. I declare that His peace will rise within you like a river—unstoppable, unshakable, and overflowing. Every wound, every unanswered question, every storm must bow to the Prince of Peace who reigns within you. You carry His glory. His peace will guide you into divine appointments, uncommon favor, and victorious battles.

I commission you to live from a place of spiritual rest, fully anchored in the sovereignty of God.

I commission you to live a life of worship—in spirit, in truth, and in power. Let your life be a living testimony of the transformation that comes from surrendering to Him.

I commission you to walk out the peace you've received. Let it spill over into your relationships, your work, and your community. Be the peacemaker you were created to be, bringing the hope of Christ into every conversation, every encounter, and every moment.

I commission you as a warrior of peace—armed with the Word, led by the Spirit, and rooted in the love of the Father. Go forth to restore what has been broken, reclaim what the enemy has stolen, and release the captives into the freedom of Christ. You are anointed to proclaim the good news, bind up the brokenhearted, and declare the year of the Lord's favor.

Go forth as an ambassador of peace, grounded in His presence, equipped with His Word, and empowered by His Spirit. Trust in His covenant, walk in His authority, and let His peace restore and transform every area of your life. The journey of peace is not over—it has only just begun. As you remain in Him, you will be equipped for every step of the call, and His peace will go before you, making your path straight.

Prayer of Commissioning

Lord Jesus, You are the Prince of Peace, the One who calms storms with a single word and dispels darkness with light.

I ask that You fill every heart with Your unshakeable peace and ignite in us a boldness to step confidently into the unknown. May Your Word be a fire within us, Your peace be our shield, and Your Spirit be our guiding light.

Holy Spirit, refine me, empower me, and help me walk in holiness every day. Father, please help me find opportunities to shine Your light and embody Your holiness in my work, home, and community. May I serve as an ambassador for Your kingdom, reflecting Your glory in all that I do.

I now go forth, armed with Your peace and empowered by Your Spirit, to do the impossible, to see the invisible, and to conquer in Your name.

For Your glory and by Your power—in Jesus' name. Amen.

Reference List

Pitre, Isaac. *Take Back Your Authority: Kingdom Keys to Overthrowing the Powers of Darkness*. Shippensburg, PA: Destiny Image Publishers, Inc, 2023.

Reese, Andy, Jennifer Barnett, and Neil Anderson. *Freedom Tools: For Overcoming Life's Tough Problems*. Grand Rapids: Chosen Books, 2015.

Taylor, Ford. *Relactional Leadership: When Relationships Collide with Transactions: Practical Tools for Every Leader*. Houston, Texas.: High Bridge Books, 2021.

Appendix A

Prayer for Refinement

Lord, I come before You today, asking You to refine me and purify my heart. I acknowledge Your role in transforming me into the likeness of Christ, and I surrender my desires, fears, and weaknesses to You. Empower me to live a life of holiness, aligning my thoughts, actions, and attitudes with Your truth.

I pray for the grace to anchor my identity in Christ daily, remembering that I am holy because of Jesus' sacrifice. Help me embrace my new identity as a child of God, and may this truth guide my decisions and actions. Show me the hidden places in my heart where I need to pursue holiness and give me the courage to surrender those areas to You, knowing that You see and reward what's done in secret.

Help me capture my thoughts, Holy Spirit, and renew my mind. Teach me to take every thought captive and replace negativity with the truth of Your Word. May Your peace guard my mind and heart, and may I reflect Your holiness in everything I think, say, and do.

Give me the mind of Christ, Holy Spirit. Sharpen my discernment and help me to make decisions that align with Your will. I want to walk in radical obedience, no matter how big or small the steps. Help me to immediately obey Your nudges, trusting that Your ways lead to peace and holiness.

Lord, I also embrace the power of repentance. When I fall short, help me to quickly turn to You, confessing my sins and receiving Your forgiveness. Let repentance become a daily practice that keeps me in alignment with Your holiness and draws me closer to You.

I pray that Your holiness influences every relationship I have. Show me where I need to seek forgiveness, love, and purity in my interactions with others. May I be an instrument of Your peace and grace in every relationship I encounter.

Lord, help me to cultivate a lifestyle of worship in every moment. May my life be a constant offering to You, and may I surrender every action, word, and thought as an act of worship. Let Your holiness flow through me in every area of my life.

Finally, I pray that You will show me how to live with the higher calling of peace. Reveal opportunities for me to shine Your light and represent Your holiness in my work, home, and community. May I live as an ambassador for Your kingdom, reflecting Your glory in all I do.

Holy Spirit, refine me, empower me, and guide me to walk in holiness, peace, and the fruit of Your Spirit each day. In Jesus' name, Amen!

Prayer to Receive the Gift of Tongues

Father God, I come to You in faith, knowing that You are a good Father who delights in giving good gifts to those who ask. Your Word says that if I ask, You will give the Holy Spirit to those who seek You (Luke 11:9–13). I thank You for the gift of the Holy Spirit, who empowers and guides me.

I ask, Lord, to be baptized with the Holy Spirit, as You promised in Your Word (Acts 1:4–5). I open my heart to receive the gift of speaking in tongues. I believe that through this gift, the Spirit will help me pray according to Your will (Romans 8:26–27) and that I will be able to speak mysteries to You (1 Corinthians 14:2).

I trust this gift is for my spiritual growth, and I believe the Holy Spirit will pray through me according to Your perfect will. Just as the early believers were filled with the Holy Spirit and began to speak in other tongues (Acts 2:4), I now receive this powerful manifestation of Your presence.

Lord, I surrender my will to You completely. I humble myself before You and ask for forgiveness—for any sin in my life or in my family line that may have blocked the flow of Your Spirit. I renounce every false agreement, every form of witchcraft, every sin, and anything that has stood in the way of receiving all You have for me.

I ask You now to fill me afresh with Your Holy Spirit. I receive the gift of tongues by faith, not by striving, but by trusting in Your goodness and Your Word. I believe this gift will strengthen my spirit, build me up in faith, and draw me into deeper communion with You.

Thank You, Father, for this powerful gift of edification, intercession, and intimate worship. I yield to Your Spirit now and choose to walk in full surrender. Let my tongue be an instrument of praise, power, and prayer—released for Your glory.

In Jesus' mighty name, Amen.

Now, start practicing: As you begin to speak in tongues, trust the Holy Spirit to guide you. Don't worry about how it sounds—speak in faith, knowing that the Spirit is interceding for you in alignment with God's will. Take a step of obedience and let the Spirit flow through you.

Embracing Freedom in Christ

Inner Healing Prayer

Welcome to your journey of inner healing. This guide is a sacred invitation to experience the transformative love and freedom that Jesus offers to all His children. No matter where you've been, what you've faced, or what wounds you carry, you are about to embark on a path that will lead you closer to God's heart and to the full restoration He desires for you.

The truth is that Jesus has already won the victory for you on the cross. Through His sacrifice, He has made a way for you to walk in freedom—freedom from pain, lies, and the chains of your past. And this freedom is not just a distant promise; it is a present reality you can experience right now.

This guide integrates principles from my own personal healing framework, Amana Prayer, along with inspiration from Freedom Tools by Andy Reese for a Personal Self-Talk Script. You will be equipped to:

- Identify and heal emotional wounds that have shaped your life.

- Break free from lies and agreements that have kept you stuck in patterns of fear, shame, or insecurity.

- Renounce judgments that block healing and embrace forgiveness that releases you into peace.

- Step into your true identity in Christ—beloved, chosen, and empowered to live out God's purpose for your life.

This is a process of encountering Jesus—of meeting Him where you are and allowing His love to transform you from the inside out. With each prayer and declaration of truth, you will align yourself more deeply with the freedom Christ has already secured for you.

As you read this guide, I encourage you to take your time. Allow the Holy Spirit to lead you at your own pace. Know that each step brings you closer to a life of wholeness, peace, and joy. Jesus is with you every step of the way, and He longs to heal, restore, and empower you to walk in the fullness of who you are in Him.

Are you ready to step into the freedom that is already yours in Christ? Let's begin.

Preparation: Creating Sacred Space

Find a quiet, comfortable place where you can focus and be free from distractions. Take a few deep breaths and invite the Holy Spirit to guide you through this time of healing.

Center your heart, open yourself to the Lord's work, and remember that this is a moment of encounter with His transformative love.

Opening Prayer: Inviting the Presence of God

Heavenly Father, I come before You in the mighty name of Jesus Christ. I invite Your presence into this sacred moment and set this space apart for Your divine healing and restoration.

As Hebrews 4:12 declares, *"For the word of God is living and powerful, and sharper than any two-edged sword, piercing even to the division of soul and spirit, and of joints and marrow, and is a discerner of the thoughts and intents of the heart."*

Lord, I come before You in full surrender. Spirit of truth, I ask You to prepare my heart for Your healing work. Pierce through every layer—soul and spirit, thought and intention—and do what only You can do. Expose what needs to be removed. Restore what has been broken. Uproot every lie and replace it with Your truth. I trust You completely. Let Your living Word cut through the clutter of my heart and bring forth the healing and freedom I was created for.

I plead the precious blood of Jesus over my spirit, soul, and body. I renounce and break every agreement—spoken or unspoken—with fear, shame, trauma, and deception. I cancel every assignment of the enemy against my healing in Jesus' name. I command all confusion, distraction, and oppression to leave now in Jesus' name.

Holy Spirit, I fully yield to You. Take complete control of this time. Shine Your light into every wounded area of my heart. Reveal what needs healing and bring Your truth where there have been lies. Let Your love wash over every broken part of me, and let Your presence restore what has been lost.

Jesus, I declare that You alone are my Healer, my Deliverer, and my Lord. I submit to Your will and trust in Your love to make me whole. I receive Your peace and Your truth as I walk through this process with You. I trust that You are with me—guiding, protecting, and restoring me.

Thank You, Father, for Your mercy. Thank You, Jesus, for Your sacrifice. Thank You, Holy Spirit, for Your power at work within me. I receive all that You have for me now. In Jesus' name, Amen.

1. Self-Talk to Wounded Parts

I speak to all the wounded parts of me. I recognize the ways you've protected me, and I honor your role in helping me survive. But today, I choose healing so that I can walk in wholeness. You no longer need to carry these burdens, for Jesus is my Protector, and the Holy Spirit is my Comforter and Guide.

No matter your role, Jesus has something better for you. Darkness can no longer remain. The light has come. It is my will that you be healed today. I wish to serve Jesus with my whole heart. You are safe here You are seen. You are no longer alone.

I speak to the wounded parts of myself, inviting you to receive healing. I love Jesus of Nazareth, the Son of God, and I desire for every part of me to know Him and trust Him. Please go down and rest, And when I call, come forward one at a time—ready to be healed, ready to encounter the One who loves you perfectly.

2. Identifying and Healing Specific Emotions

I want to speak to the part of me that feels [name the emotion: fear, rejection, anger, sadness, etc.].

· How old was I when I first felt this way?

· What is the deepest emotion you're holding for me?

Are there other parts of me that feel this way, too? If so, I invite them to come forward."

(Pause and allow the Holy Spirit to move these parts of your heart forward, paying attention to any emotions that arise.)

3. Invite Jesus to Heal

Jesus of Nazareth, the Son of God, I invite You into these wounded places in my heart. Bring healing where I need it most. I trust You with my heart and surrender this pain to You.

Jesus...

· What do You want this parts of me to know about You?

· What do You want me to release or surrender to You?

· What do You want to speak to me today?

Pause and listen for what Jesus may be saying or doing in this healing space. Trust that He is present, speaking, and working within your heart.

4. Break Curses

In the name of Jesus, I break every curse over my life- spoken, unspoken, generational, or self-imposed. I declare that every curse is broken at the Cross. Jesus became a curse for me (Galatians 3:13), so I do not have to live under its weight.

I break the curse of [insert specific curse, such as poverty, fear, infirmity, abandonment, addiction, etc.]. I cancel its legal right to influence my life. I apply the blood of Jesus to every root and effect, and I declare freedom in His name.

Example: "I break the curse of abandonment that entered through my father walking away." "I break the generational curse of addiction passed down through my family line."

I command all spirits attached to these curses to leave now, in the name of Jesus. You no longer have a place in my life. I belong to Jesus, and I am covered by His blood.

5. Forgiveness and Release

In Jesus' name, I forgive [name] for [specific offense], which made me feel [emotion]. I forgive and release [name] into blessing. I rejoice that I no longer carry this burden.

I repent for judging [name]. I declare that judgment null and void. I break all demonic assignments attached to it, in Jesus' name.

6. Breaking Soul Ties and Ungodly Connections

In the name of Jesus, I break every ungodly spirit, soul, and body tie with [name the person or situation] that I have formed in my life. I return to [name] all that I took, and I take back all that is mine, cleansed by the blood of the Lamb. I declare that these connections no longer have a hold on me. I choose freedom in Jesus' name.

7. Healing Lies, Vows, and Agreements

In the name of Jesus, I come out of agreement with every lie and generational lie spoken or unspoken that has shaped or wounded me. I renounce the lie that: _____ (pause and name it). I reject it, revoke it, and break its power in Jesus' name. I no longer believe this lie. I no longer live from it. I am healed and free in Jesus' name. I close the door to the lie, and I open my heart to receive the truth.

Jesus, what is Your truth? What do You want me to know? (Pause. Listen. Let His voice speak peace, identity, and life.)

By faith, I receive Your truth. I come into full agreement with You, Jesus. I align my heart, mind, and emotions with what You say about me. I break every contract, consequence, and hidden agreement with darkness. I walk in freedom.

Examples of common lies: "I am too much." "I'm not enough." "No one will ever love me." "God has forgotten me."

Examples of inner vows: "I will never trust anyone again." "I'll take care of myself." "I won't feel anything anymore."

After each step, pause and ask Jesus if anything else needs to be addressed before moving forward.

8. Receiving the Truth and New Identity

Jesus, I open my heart to receive the truth You speak over me. How do You see me? What do You think about me? What is my identity in You?

(Pause. Listen for His voice–gentle, kind, and full of love.)

I choose to believe Your truth over every lie. I declare:

"I am who You say I am." "I am loved, accepted, and secure in You." "I am no longer defined by what has happened to me, but by what You've done for me."

Seal this truth in my heart, Jesus. Help me to live according to the identity You've given me. Let it take root and bear fruit. I align myself with Your Word, Your love, and Your purpose for my life. I am Yours.

9. Filling with the Holy Spirit

Holy Spirit, I ask You to fill every part of my heart and soul that needs healing. Come and fill me with Your peace, joy, and love. Empower me to embrace the fullness of what You have for me. Help me walk in Your freedom and live out my new identity in Christ.

10. Seal the Healing Work

Lord, thank You for the healing You have done today. I seal this work in Your name, Jesus. I declare that I am free from the wounds of my past and commit to living in the truth of who You say I am. I choose to walk in Your peace, love, and freedom. Thank You for restoring me. In Jesus' name, amen.

Final Reflection

Take a moment to reflect on the process. If anything else comes to mind, share it with the Lord and continue to trust Him with your heart's healing. After this emotional work, drink water, rest, and take care of yourself.

If you need help with any of these steps or would like to book a personal healing session, please contact Leah at https://linktr.ee/Leahboatright

About The Author

Leah Boatright is a passionate business and ministry coach and the visionary founder of Amana Prayer. This transformative ministry model integrates elements of Freedom Tools, Prophetic Heart Healing, and Life Coaching into a unique and impactful approach. Through this method, Leah guides individuals toward deeper intimacy with God, helping them ascend to the "Mountain of the Lord," where they can receive divine blueprints, clarity, and direction for their lives with clean hands and pure hearts.

Leah has successfully guided numerous individuals to overcome personal challenges and achieve spiritual breakthroughs. Her approach provides clarity and direction and has been instrumental in transforming lives.

After experiencing God's transformative peace in her own life, Leah became passionate about helping others encounter the same. With over 15 years of ministry experience and 8 years of running a homeschool co-op, Leah brings a wealth of wisdom, compassion, and practical insight into her coaching and teaching. As the host of the Lean In with Leah broadcast, Leah inspires and empowers her audience to hear Jesus' voice and align their lives with His eternal perspective. Her greatest joy is witnessing lives trans-formed through the Word of God as she coaches, teaches, and walks alongside others in their healing and spiritual growth. Leah is passionate about making Christ known worldwide, and her work reflects her deep commitment to fostering personal encounters with God—one life-changing moment at a time. Connect with Leah at https://linktr.e e/Leahboatright to join the journey toward peace and pur-pose.